The Freshwater Angler™

MODERN METHODS OF
ICE FISHING

BY TOM GRUENWALD

CREATIVE
PUBLISHING
international

MINNETONKA, MINNESOTA

TOM GRUENWALD handles product research and development for HT Enterprises, Inc., one of the world's foremost authorities and producers of ice tackle. Gruenwald, a University of Wisconsin Stevens Point Fisheries graduate, regularly writes ice-fishing articles for dozens of outdoor magazines.

DAVE GENZ led the modern ice-fishing revolution. Known by many anglers as "Mr. Ice Fishing," he invented the Fish Trap ice shelter and pioneered the use of electronics to find and catch winter fish.

CREATIVE PUBLISHING international

Chairman: Iain Macfarlane
President/CEO: David D. Murphy
Vice President/Retail Sales & Marketing: James Knapp
Creative Director: Lisa Rosenthal

MODERN METHODS OF ICE FISHING
By Tom Gruenwald

Executive Editor, Outdoor Products Group: Don Oster
Senior Editor and Project Leader: David R. Maas
Technical Advisor: Dave Genz
Managing Editor: Jill Anderson
Associate Creative Director: Bradley Springer
Senior Art Director: David Schelitzche
Photo Researcher: Angie Hartwell
Desktop Publishing Specialists: Joe Fahey, Laurie Kristensen
Staff Photographers: Tate Carlson, Andrea Rugg
Photo Assistant: David L. Tieszen
Production Manager: Stasia Dorn
Cover Photograph: Bill Lindner Photography
Contributing Photographers: Dave Genz, Mike Hehner, Mark Kayser, Bill Lindner Photography, Steve Maas, Jim Schollmeyer
Illustrators: Maynard Reece, David Schelitzche, Joseph R. Tomelleri, Jon Q. Wright
Contributing Manufacturers: Bay De Noc Lure Co. – Anders Nyberg; Berkley; Cabela's, Inc. – Jim Beardsley, Kellie Hawkins; Cobra Electronics Corporation; Cortland Line Co., Inc. – Gregg Thorne; Feldmann Engineering and Mfg. Co., Inc./Jiffy Ice Drills; Fishing Hot Spots, Inc. – Linda Garber, Mike Michalak; Fiskars Inc. – Matt Foster; HT Enterprises, Inc. – Paul F. Grahl; Mustang Survival, Inc. – Annette Baker; Nature Vision/Aqua-Vu; Normark Corporation – Craig Weber; O. Mustad & Son, Inc.; Outdoor Creations, Inc. – Ty Caswell; Reef Runner Tackle Co., Inc.; Schrader Design/ReadyRig – Bill Schrader; Shimano American Corporation; StrikeMaster Corporation – Ray Peterson; Thorne Brothers Fishing Specialty Store – Bill Fiebranz, Paul Gausman, Chris Hansen, Greg Kaasa, Lonnie Murphy, Dave Wells; USL Products Inc./Fish Trap Ice Shelter – Dennis Clark; Vexilar, Inc. – Mitchell Bennis; Zercom Marine

Contributing Individuals and Agencies: Adventure North Resort – Chip Leer; Banks Inc. – Dave Fuller; Don Coffey Company – Trevor Sumptin; Gardner Sales Associates, Inc. – Gunnar Miesen; Jay Mahs; Sokol & Associates – Steve Hauge; Team Fish Farmers – Paul Bernard, Dan Boedigheimer, Bill Botzet, Randy Bruska, Jay Carroll, Bob Ebsen, Chris Gulden, Greg Gulden, Scott Gulden, Steve Maas, Mike Wicken; Timber Valley Associates – Brian Tommerdahl

Copyright © 1999 by Creative Publishing international, Inc.
5900 Green Oak Drive
Minnetonka, MN 55343
1-800-328-3895

Library of Congress Cataloging-in-Publication Data

Gruenwald, Tom.
    Modern methods of ice fishing / by Tom Gruenwald.
       p.   cm. -- (The freshwater angler)
    ISBN 0-86573-071-7 (hardcover)
    1. Ice fishing.   I. Title.   II. Series: Hunting & fishing library.   Freshwater angler.
    SH455.45.G786   1999
    799.1'22--dc21   99-23421

Table of Contents

Introduction

Ice fishing is one of winter's most mysterious, exciting and fastest growing sports. This book, *Modern Methods of Ice Fishing*, helps you learn the sport of ice fishing, inside and out, front to back. First, you'll learn how fish use their senses to survive in their frigid winter environment, what they eat, and how they respond to various environments beneath the ice throughout the winter. From here, you'll see how to dress for the conditions, what equipment and gear is needed to get started in this sport, and how hydrographic lake maps, navigation equipment and sonar devices help you find fish hidden beneath thick layers of ice.

The real "heart" of the book is the section titled, "Winter Gamefish Techniques." It covers the basic winter patterns necessary to find and catch all of winter's most popular species, including sunfish, crappies, walleyes, saugers, yellow perch, northern pike, lake trout, stream trout, tullibee and even burbot. Each of the chapters in this section begins by introducing a species and a brief description of how to identify it, then shows you where you will be most likely to find the species throughout the winter on several types of waters, and the most prominent times to fish for them. Plenty of expert advice and tips are provided for each species, including some insights from noted ice-fishing guru Dave Genz. As inventor of the Fish Trap ice shelter and many other truly innovative ice-fishing products, Dave passes on his winter secrets gained from over 40 years of following the hottest ice bites across northern North America.

The book concludes with how to properly care and prepare your catches destined for the frying pan, and how to maintain their maximum freshness until you're ready to cook. And for those fish intended for release, you'll see the proper procedures for handling fish to maximize their chances of survival.

The real secret to icing more fish is knowledge, and *Modern Methods of Ice Fishing* provides all the background information, insights, and knowledge necessary to be a successful winter angler. The only thing that teaches you more is time on the ice.

Above all, as you learn this great sport, remember that the future of fishing is in the hands of our youth. So this winter, take the time to show a child how to fish. You'll be rewarded many times over when you see the joy in their eyes as that first fish is held for a photograph.

Ice-Fishing Opportunities

While ice fishing is primarily a sport of Canada and the northern United States, some regionalized pockets of high elevation ice fishing takes place in some quite surprising southern areas, including places such as Nevada, northeast Arizona and north central New Mexico.

On the accompanying illustration, the primary ice fishing climate in North America is covered by the winter photograph. (While Alaska and much of Canada aren't featured on the map, these areas are obviously hotbeds of ice fishing for several months each year.) The light blue region bordering the bottom edge of the photograph depicts a window of only limited ice-fishing opportunity, where ice fishing is typically available during only the coldest portion of the winter, or during exceptionally cold winters.

The dark blue pockets shown in northern California, northeast Arizona and north central New Mexico are areas often receiving ice cover during the winter, but only on limited waters. Many of the waters in these areas subject to freezing are found only at high elevations, so obtaining access to these often remote, alpine waters is limited to only the most adventuresome and resourceful winter anglers.

Winter anglers are, however, a mobile, adventuresome breed. Serious winter anglers make it a point to travel into parts of Canada, northern North Dakota, Minnesota or Wisconsin in late November and early December, where ice may have frozen several inches thick before any ice formation at all has occurred across the central or southern portions of the North American ice-fishing region. When ice thickens and fish activity slows in these areas, anglers gradually move south, following the initial ice formation and with it, the classic better fishing action often found during the so-called "first-ice" period.

The opposite phenomena occurs in late winter as the ice begins melting along the southern edges of the region. During this period, hard-core fishermen gradually move north, again, trying to extend their

High-Elevation Ice Regions

ice-fishing season while at the same time spending more time fishing during the classic, good fishing action often displayed during the so-called "late-ice" period.

This may sound like a lot of movement and travel, and it is; however, one distinct advantage of ice fishing is its relative economics. Compared to summer travel, there's no expensive boat needed, no pricey gasoline bills from running a large outboard motor, and no extra time needed to prep such rigs, lessening the additional costs and headaches involved with trailering a large rig.

The sensible economics of ice fishing can be taken even further when you consider that even when fishing from the largest bass and walleye boats, the total

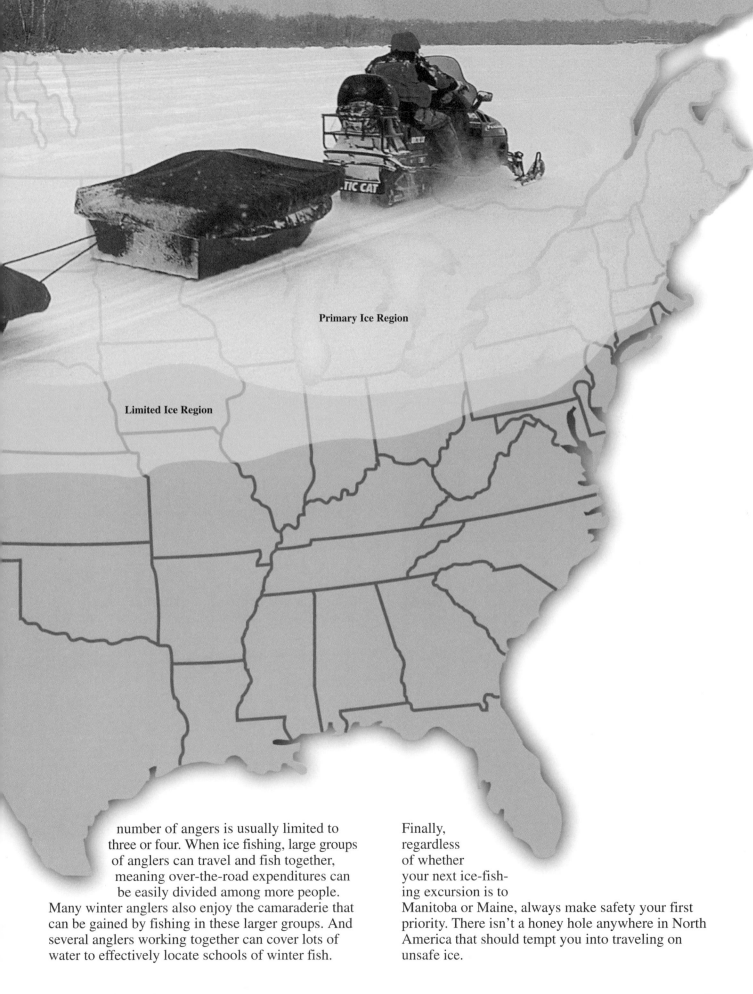

Primary Ice Region

Limited Ice Region

number of angers is usually limited to three or four. When ice fishing, large groups of anglers can travel and fish together, meaning over-the-road expenditures can be easily divided among more people. Many winter anglers also enjoy the camaraderie that can be gained by fishing in these larger groups. And several anglers working together can cover lots of water to effectively locate schools of winter fish.

Finally, regardless of whether your next ice-fishing excursion is to Manitoba or Maine, always make safety your first priority. There isn't a honey hole anywhere in North America that should tempt you into traveling on unsafe ice.

Ice-Fishing Safety

The primary consideration before beginning any ice-fishing trek is ice thickness. To be safe, you need 3 inches of solid ice for walking; 4 for ice fishing; 5 for walking on ice with a heavy load of gear; 7 for a loaded snowmobile or ATV; 8 for a car or light truck; and 12 for a large truck.

Air temperatures must be sustained beneath the freezing point to form ice, and the colder the temperature, the deeper and faster ice forms. As a result, lakes farther north usually freeze first. While many beginning anglers realize the importance of geographic location and temperature in ice formation, they don't understand that a variety of other conditions influence ice thickness, including a lake's depth and shape.

Shallow lakes, yielding less volume than deep ones, cool faster and thus freeze sooner. They also warm faster, and consequently experience ice-out sooner than their slower cooling, deeper counterparts.

Man-made lakes featuring a flow of water

are not only subject to fluctuating ice thicknesses, but fluctuating water levels that may cause deteriorating ice conditions. And since most man-make lakes are also longer and narrower than natural lakes, they're subjected to special sets of conditions. When shallow and protected from the wind and sun, they may freeze earlier in winter. If deep and exposed to the primary winds and open to the sun, this combination of factors plus current flow may cause them to freeze much later.

On any body of water, periods of locally warming weather, especially those featuring rain to erode the ice and increase runoff, decrease ice thickness. Moving currents caused by incoming rivers, springs, flocks of geese or ducks, or even schools of fish swimming under the ice may have similar results. Another thing to watch out for is emergent weeds, which absorb the sun's warmth and decrease the thickness of the surrounding ice. Similarly, in late winter the shoreline warms quickly once all the snow is melted, making the ice near shore much thinner and weaker than mid-lake ice.

Here are several situations anglers should be aware of before venturing out onto the ice:

NEW ICE VS. OLD ICE. Clear blue, freshly formed ice is much stronger than old ice that has been partially thawed or broken up and refrozen.

LAKE NARROWS. Unprotected, weedy, dark-bottom narrows between lakes or lake basins are often shallow and subject to current flow, inhibiting ice formation.

RIVER CURRENTS. River ice varies greatly in thickness, depending on the channel depth, bottom content and current velocity.

SPRINGS. Inflowing springs bring warmer, moving water that can create pockets of open water or thin ice.

ICE CRACKS, HEAVES AND RIDGES. Anglers should avoid pressure cracks, heaves and ridges. Such areas form when layers of thickening ice expand, often leaving lines of open water that may expand as winds shift the ice.

SAFETY EQUIPMENT

Along with the knowledge of the many factors that affect ice thickness, you should be prepared for the unexpected by carrying the following safety items:

LIFE JACKET. Few summer anglers would consider leaving the dock without life jackets on or at least handy, yet will walk out on ice of unknown thickness unprotected. Whenever possible, wear a Coast Guard-approved personal floatation device (PFD) when traveling on ice of questionable thickness.

CHISEL. As you walk onto any frozen lake, check ice thickness by striking it firmly with a sharp chisel. If the chisel punctures or cracks the ice, immediately follow your path back to shore.

ICE CLEATS. Ice cleats, or creepers, consist of adjustable straps, belts, elastic bands or rubber over-shoes supporting metal teeth. They attach to boots, allowing traction on smooth, slippery ice, helping anglers avoid injury-causing falls.

Ice cleats

Ice picks

ICE PICKS. Ice anglers venturing on ice of unknown thickness should always carry ice picks. Should you fall through thin ice, the picks can be stuck into the ice and used to pull yourself from the icy waters.

ROPE. Ice anglers should also carry a rope in a convenient location, so in the unfortunate situation someone falls through, you can offer them "assistance from a distance." A rope may also help if you should fall through, as you can toss one end to your potential rescuer.

As a rule, you should always inquire about ice conditions with knowledgeable, local people familiar with your waters before leaving shore. Above all, use common sense and intuition. If you feel the ice may not be solid enough to fish on, don't take any unnecessary chances. STAY OFF!

Flotation Suits

Although personal floatation devices (PFDs) are just starting to catch on in many parts of the United States, many experienced ice anglers in Canada wear "flotation" or "antihypothermia" suits. While these suits are expensive, they may save your life should you break through the ice.

One of the best flotation suits on the market today is the Mustang® antiexposure coverall (left). This high-tech suit is lined with Airsoft PVC closed cell foam, which provides both buoyancy and insulation. Other features include: neoprene wrist closures for weather proofness; Tug-Tites at thighs and ankles for improved fit; hand warmer and cargo pockets at hips; and head support pillow for additional flotation. This coverall is worn almost exclusively by the U.S. Coast Guard.

For more information on flotation suits, call Mustang Survival at 360-676-1782 or visit their website at www.mustangsurvival.com

Understanding Fish & Their
Winter Environment

Fish Senses

Although fish are cold-blooded and slowed down metabolically in the winter, many species remain active beneath the ice; a few studies have even suggested some cold-water species may become more aggressive in winter than during the open-water season, feeding just as much or more than other periods of the year.

Obviously winter fish must adapt to their icy world, learning to continue moving, feeding and detecting danger. These things are accomplished through vision, hearing, smell, taste and a unique vibration sensing series of cells unique to fish called the *lateral line*.

LATERAL LINE. This long band of fluid-filled nerve endings help fish not only detect sudden water movement that may help them avoid danger, but even sense minute vibrations sent out by struggling prey that might help them target an easy meal. The lateral line also helps fish determine the size, speed and direction of both predators and prey, and locate stationery objects beneath the ice.

Anyone who has ever marveled at the way huge schools of baitfish swim uniformly in motion, even when disturbed, should realize it's the sensitive and responsive nerve endings of the lateral line that allow this incredible synchronous, fluid motion.

VISION. Fish also sense light intensity, and while the spectrum may be limited in some species or those holding in deep water, many fish can also detect color. Even when fish can't differentiate a specific color, they can still identify vibrations with their lateral lines and use their eyes to note flashes of irregular light intensity to home in on the target. Once there, the size, shape and profile of the item will appear, not in full color perhaps, but at least as varying shades of grey.

The distance fish can see is dependent on light intensity and water clarity. In ultra-clear environments during bright days, fish may be able to see several feet away, while in turbid water at night, vision may be limited to only a few inches. But thanks to winter's icy ceiling, water clarity often improves as winds no longer stir the water, and as sunlight penetration is eventually reduced, algae growth is reduced as well, helping to further improve clarity.

Lateral line

From a winter angler's standpoint, these conditions mean fish can see our lures and baits well, and since these presentations are vertically set in place, fish have ample time to examine and review our offerings, which is why lighter, more precise techniques are often required to trigger strikes beneath the ice.

Fish can also see overhead objects quite well, so it's important to not cast fast moving objects or shadows over cut holes, or you're likely to spook fish. Even when thick ice and deep snow help conceal your presence, it can be a good idea to set the depths of your lures and baits above your target fish, where they might be easier for winter fish to find.

HEARING. While fish don't have external ears to hear like humans, they do have an inner ear that functions quite similarly. A series of delicate bones within the fish's head detect sound, and a series of interconnected semicircular canals allow balance. This, in association with the vibration detection capabilities of the lateral line, keeps fish well tuned with their environment. Some winter anglers believe using subtle, sound-making devices such as fins that click against lure bodies help attract fish to their baits, especially in dark water.

SMELL. Fish have a highly developed sense of smell attained through their olfactory systems. Odor is detected when water passes through small openings called *nares*, usually located just above the fish's mouth. Water enters through the front nare, runs through the nasal sac and is released through the rear nare.

Although odor is seldom used to track prey from a long distance, fish can use their sense of smell to home in on nearby food, thus ice anglers usually tip their lures with live bait or soak ice lures with fish attractants. Fish can also detect foreign odors and the odors of predators indicating danger. Many anglers, believing fish can detect the water-borne odor of a human, use fish attractants to mask human odors.

TASTE. Few winter anglers can deny the importance of adding the natural scent, texture and taste of live bait to an ice-fishing presentation. Winter fish can certainly be caught without the use of natural bait or a derivative thereof, but they are rare. Most winter catches require at least the taste of live bait to enhance the effectiveness of the presentation.

HOW SENSES AFFECT ICE-FISHING STRATEGIES. Knowledge of these senses will certainly help improve your fishing. Ice pros, for example, avoid scraping portable ice shacks across the ice, especially when fishing shallow, clear water during first ice, knowing fish can easily be spooked by the unnatural sound and vibration.

Many anglers use long rods when fishing clear, shallow water to decrease the chance of being seen. And as we've already reviewed, some ice anglers add colored beads or spinners to add color and flash to their presentations, helping attract fish by sight. Others use rattles to add fish-attracting vibrations, and almost all knowledgeable ice anglers have realized the importance of using live bait to add fish-attracting scent, taste and texture to their winter presentations.

Nares

Winter Foods

Winter poses many challenges for fish, and a primary one is forage availability. With most popular winter species spawning during spring, fish eggs are long gone by ice-up, and the number of vulnerable, easily captured fry and baitfish have been lowered considerably by predation through the long open-water season. Insect hatches have ceased. Leeches are virtually nonexistent. Runoff is limited, restricting incoming nutrients for phytoplankton growth, and as snow piles atop thickening ice, sunlight penetration is reduced, further lowering the number of phytoplankton and limiting the zooplankton that depend on them for food. Invertebrate numbers are also reduced, with important prey items like crayfish often not as abundant as during the open-water season.

Fortunately, fish are cold-blooded, so their metabolism is greatly slowed in winter, reducing their need for food. Yet at the same time, winter fish still must feed, and they do find forage from all parts of the food chain available. Numerous species of phytoplankton and zooplankton, panfish fry, invertebrates such as freshwater shrimp, scuds (and in some environments, the newly introduced exotic zebra mussels), aquatic insect larvae such as mayfly nymphs, aquatic worms and a variety of minnows all provide winter prey for fish beneath the ice. And because this winter prey is often small and slow, they're vulnerable to predation.

Depending on availability, abundance, competition with other feeding species and how opportunistic or hungry winter fish are, they may choose or be forced to feed upon any one or all the following forage species throughout the winter:

PHYTOPLANKTON, or tiny, mostly microscopic plants, comprise the base of the winter aquatic food pyramid. When sunlight penetration is adequate, especially during first and late ice, phytoplankton are readily available and provide a consistent food source for smaller baitfish and panfish.

ZOOPLANKTON are tiny, mostly microscopic animals that feed on phytoplankton, and are often found in the same areas as phytoplankton. They are also readily available in winter and provide stable forage for panfish.

FLATS, or tiny panfish fry, primarily sunfish, perch and crappies, are hatched in spring and grow large enough to provide a common winter food source for many gamefish.

INSECT LARVAE, such as midge and caddis larvae, and mayfly nymphs, such as the hex, are often available to winter fish and comprise significant portions of their diets. Mayfly nymphs are commonly referred to as "wigglers" by many winter anglers.

INVERTEBRATES, such as crayfish, freshwater shrimp and snails, are all important winter foods

even though they may be limited in availability depending on the environment.

TUBIFICID WORMS, commonly called "blood worms" by many winter anglers, live on deep, muddy, oxygen-scarce flats. As oxygen concentrations decline, they project their tubelike breathing apparatus into the water to increase surface area for absorbing oxygen. The farther their bodies stick out, the easier they are for fish to prey upon.

BAITFISH AND MINNOWS, such as shiners and shad, provide food for many types of large gamefish.

SCHOOLING PANFISH, such as sunfish, perch, smelt and cisco, provide a staple portion of the diet for large gamefish.

FROGS may reappear from their semidormant winter state during the late-ice period and become subject to predation.

HOW FOOD AFFECTS WINTER FISH LOCATION AND BEHAVIOR. Often, winter fish feed upon a preferred or the most readily available forage, and consequently, are attracted to areas holding these food items. Walleyes feeding on shad, for example, would be likely found feeding on suspended schools of shad holding over open water, while walleyes feeding on small perch might be found on weedy flats or deep, hard-bottom structure. At the same time, perch feeding on plankton would probably be found in shallow weeds or suspended over open water, while those feeding on bloodworms would likely hold on deep mud flats.

Fish Activity Under the Ice

Water temperature is important to fish, and obviously a concern in winter, because it's basically one thing: cold. Winter water temperatures vary only from slightly above the freezing point at 33°F just below the ice, to 39°F, the maximum density of water, at lake bottom. Since fish are cold-blooded, their activity beneath the ice is slowed by this cold, simply because the colder water reduces their metabolism, limiting their requirement for food and oxygen intake as well.

However, while their requirements for food and oxygen are more limited, fish still must satisfy their basic needs for shelter, food and oxygen, and it's these three factors that most often dictate fish location and activity beneath the ice.

SHELTER is just as important beneath the ice as it is in summer, because it provides a place for winter fish to hide from predators and ambush prey. Natural cover such as weeds, logs and rocks or man-made items such as dock pilings or fish cribs all attract winter fish.

FOOD is also important. Although fish seldom eat as much or as often in winter due to their reduced metabolism, they still feed and actively search for locations offering the most abundant, preferred forms of prey.

OXYGEN. The water fish inhabit must also feature sufficient oxygen counts to meet a species' minimum requirements. While some species such as pike, crappies and perch can withstand lower oxygen conditions than many species, others such as lake trout, salmon and whitefish demand highly oxygenated waters for survival. All species seek locations meeting their basic oxygen needs.

SEASONAL MOVEMENTS

The three basic needs for shelter, food and oxygen are all highly dependent on a lake's size, depth, fertility, variety and type of structure and cover, ability to sustain dissolved oxygen counts, water clarity and the presence of current. Throughout the winter, fish seek specific locations that come closest to satisfying all their individual needs, and these vary in different environments.

Shallow, muck-bottom lakes, for example, tend to be fertile, dingy and become oxygen starved beneath the ice, thereby restricting fish movement. Large, deep, rocky lakes tend to be relatively infertile, clear and sustain good oxygen counts throughout the winter, allowing fish more movement and a greater variety of location options.

SMALL, SHALLOW LAKES. In early winter, just as ice-up occurs, fish may be found at virtually any depth, but tend to hold in the deepest holes where the water is warmest and most chemically stable.

By midwinter, thickening ice and deep snow reduce the amount of sunlight reaching vegetation, limiting the plants' ability to produce oxygen, forcing fish into depth zones supplying more suitable oxygen concentration. As fish are forced from their preferred areas of shelter and food, they become stressed and feed less.

Late in the winter, if thick ice and deep snow completely block sunlight, photosynthesis and plant oxygen-producing capabilities ceases entirely. Vegetation dies, reducing shelter availability, and plant decomposition uses dissolved oxygen, further restricting available oxygen in the shallows and deep water, often forcing fish to suspend just beneath the ice over deep water. Winter fish now focus more on survival than feeding, and fishing can become difficult. If this situation persists to where the band of limited oxygen becomes too large or overcomes the entire lake, the fish may die, causing a situation called *winterkill*.

LARGE, DEEP LAKES. At first ice, fish may be found in deep holes, on mid-depth humps, or on shallow flats or points. The warm, stable water in the depths, however, tends to hold the most fish.

By midwinter, deep snow and thickening ice reduce the amount of sunlight reaching into the depths, but since oxygen concentrations aren't dependent on photosynthesis and remain relatively high, fish can hold deep, move freely into shallower water or suspend. Fish location now becomes less dependent on oxygen and more dependent on subtle water temperature variations, the accessibility of shelter and availability of food.

Late in the winter, very thick ice and deep snow may completely block sunlight, especially in the depths, but oxygen concentrations are still likely to remain strong simply because the sheer volume of deep, cold water had ample oxygen available to begin with, and since no decaying vegetation uses additional dissolved oxygen, oxygen concentrations are maintained and fish can move about as they wish. Again, location patterns are dictated largely by subtle temperature variations, shelter and forage availability.

Seasonal Movement in a Small, Shallow Lake

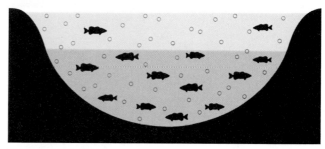

EARLY WINTER. Ice forms on a cold, still night, though the lake may reopen if milder days return. Fish may be found at any depth, but most stay in deep water where the temperature is warmer.

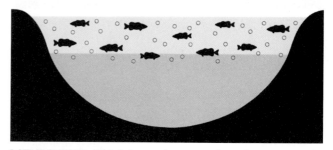

MIDWINTER. Thick ice and snow reduce the amount of sunlight reaching aquatic plants, so they cease to produce oxygen. Decaying plants and animals on the bottom consume oxygen, forcing fish to the oxygen-rich shallows.

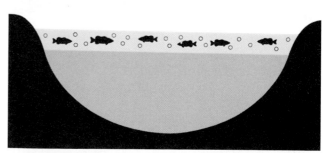

LATE WINTER. Ice and snow cover grows thicker. The low oxygen band widens. Soon, only the extreme upper layer has enough oxygen. A late winter thaw may bring oxygen into the lake. If not, it winterkills.

NORTHERN PIKE feed much more during the day than they do at night.

similar. Given bright, high-pressure conditions, fish tend to feed less actively than during overcast, low pressure conditions. Some ice anglers believe this is due to increased air pressure on a fish's air bladder. Others feel the increased light penetration during the clear, blue-bird skies of a cold front sends fish into periods of inactivity. However, while periods of activity are seldom as intense as twilight or evening bites, provided oxygen is sufficient, thick ice, deep snow or darkened water clarity may allow limited daytime feeding. Either way, ice anglers agree weather has a solid impact on fish activity beneath the ice.

STRUCTURE is essentially the formation of the lake bottom. Lakes that are simply bowl-shaped offer very little topography change to draw fish into specific areas. Lakes featuring numerous rifts, kettles and ridges offer fish a wider variety of depth, oxygen, shelter and forage options. Devout ice anglers understand such locations offering the best selection of shelter, food and oxygen are likely to draw the most fish.

Seasonal movements are further influenced by three other important factors: light, weather and current.

LIGHT-sensitive species such as walleyes and saugers have their winter movements strongly influenced by light penetration. In a deep, clear lake where light penetration is good, for example, winter walleyes are more likely to feed in deep water while light is progressively filtered out, or shallow under the cover of darkness. If ice and snow cover becomes thick enough to shade incoming light, however, they may move shallower or feed during the day, depending on shelter and forage availability. In a shallow, dingy lake where light penetration is limited, winter walleyes may still feed during low-light periods, but might be more inclined to feed longer in the morning and begin earlier in the afternoon.

WEATHER. Most anglers understand the influence of weather on fish in summer, and winter response is

COVER. Structures offering the most cover, including weeds, rocks, wood or man-made features that draw forage and provide shelter from predators and ambush points to attack prey will generally be most productive, provided oxygen levels are sufficient, food is available and the weather and light conditions are suitable.

CURRENT is another important under-ice factor, as current flow from an outside, open-water source brings oxygen and attracts food. And since current in shallow water impedes ice formation, green vegetation may persist longer in such areas, providing cover and further increasing oxygen counts.

DAILY MOVEMENTS

Serious ice anglers striving to achieve consistency keep open minds and spend a great deal of time pondering each lake's variety of shelter, food, oxygen, structure, cover and current options. Then, they consider daily factors such as weather and light, and try to figure what variety of daily conditions offers the best feeding options for the species they're trying to catch. From here, they test their theories in an attempt to better understand fish movements beneath the ice.

These anglers have established some basic, daily patterns for locating winter fish. Walleyes and crappies, for example, are light-sensitive species and consequently are most active during low-light or evening periods. They've also been found to be better adapted to feeding during these times than many species, so they also gain a competitive advantage over competitors trying to capture the same meal—and a fish-catching advantage to anglers "in the know."

Although pike and perch are certainly likely to hold tight to cover or in deep water during midday, they are much more prone to feed throughout the day, even on clear lakes during bright conditions. This may be because competing species such as walleyes and crappies are less active during these periods, providing pike and perch with a distinct feeding advantage of their own.

Fish may also move back and forth from shallow to deep water on a daily basis, usually only moving shallow during periods most conducive to efficient feeding and deeper during periods of inactivity, but they prefer not to move far. This is why cover adjacent to deep water often holds more winter fish than cover far removed from drop-offs and located far up onto remote, shallow flats. Some species also rise higher in the water column at night, when light penetration is reduced; a few savvy anglers have even discovered active fish suspended and feeding just beneath the ice while night fishing.

WALLEYES usually feed during low-light periods.

These basic daily winter patterns can be taken a step further as anglers strive to determine not only when, but where fish are most likely to hold and where the most intense winter feeding occurs throughout the day, based on their basic needs for food, shelter and oxygen. But we'll reserve such specifics for future chapters on the individual species.

Natural Lakes

Natural lakes (above) are made up of special qualities and, properly evaluated, each characteristic can help reveal important winter fish-catching secrets. Knowing this, winter experts carefully examine a natural lake's geographic location, size, depth, shape, depth contours, water clarity and fertility prior to jaunting onto the ice. After reviewing such information, they can then classify natural lakes into one of three types: oligotrophic, mesotrophic and eutrophic, which provides clues regarding the fish species likely to be present, their abundance, their habitat, habits and behavior beneath the ice.

Oligotrophic lakes are found in infertile geographic regions such as the Canadian shield, a large expanse of rocky, sterile lands covering eastern Canada and the northern United States. Oligotrophic lakes are also found in high elevation areas. Since oligotrophic waters are found in rocky, steep, infertile lands, they're typically deep, rocky, cold and well oxygenated, lack vegetation and support mostly cold-water species such as lake trout.

Mesotrophic lakes are found in moderately fertile regions, but are most prominent in southern Canada and the northern United States. Since these lakes are moderately fertile, they're typically moderately deep, gravel and sand-bottomed waters featuring only moderate weed growth and cool water, so cool-water species such as walleyes predominate.

Eutrophic lakes are found in rich, highly fertile areas, such as agricultural regions. Since eutrophic waters are so fertile and rich in nitrogen, phosphorous and other nutrients, they're typically shallow, soft-bottomed waters featuring dense weed growth and relatively warm water, so warm-water species such as largemouth bass, sunfish and crappies predominate.

These classifications are important to an ice fisherman. Obviously, if your goal is to catch lake trout, a cold-water species, you don't want to fish fertile, eutrophic lakes; and if your goal is to catch some largemouth bass, you wouldn't likely want to fish an oligotrophic lake.

Each lake classification also offers unique combinations of factors governing winter fish habitat and behavior. Fish beneath the ice of a deep oligotrophic lake, for example, are unlikely to be weed related, simply because few weeds exist. Those in a shallow eutrophic lake, however, are likely to be strongly weed related, and hence, different sets of patterns would apply to finding these fish beneath the ice.

Oxygen-rich oligotrophic lakes seldom have oxygen depletion problems, even during midwinter, so fish can roam and feed throughout the lake basin all season. Eutrophic lakes, however, are likely to undergo dramatic winter oxygen declines, especially during exceptionally cold winters when ice and snow are thick and sunlight is blocked, causing fish to become stressed and not feed. Some lakes may even have oxygen levels reduced below the level to support fish, causing winterkill.

Ponds & Pits

Throughout North America, an amazing amount of ice fishing effort is focused on ponds (right). Perhaps this shouldn't be too surprising, considering natural and man-made ponds are found scattered across the countryside in parks, on farms, ranches and in people's "back forties" across the United States and Canada. Most ponds offering stable ice fishing are at least 15 to 20 feet deep in at least one-fourth of its area to maintain adequate oxygen and prevent winterkill. Those shallower must be aerated to supply oxygen.

Most warm-water ponds feature ample weed growth and sustain good populations of sunfish and large-mouth bass, although crappies, perch and small-mouth bass may also be present. Cold, deep, spring-fed ponds maintaining strong oxygen content beneath the ice are often stocked with stream trout, offering anglers access to some productive winter fishing opportunities.

Pits are usually differentiated from ponds by their steep drop-offs and overall depth. Usually remnants of past sand-gravel or iron mining operations, their steep, sharp breaks into deep water may run hundreds of feet deep.

Most sand or gravel quarry-style pits feature clear, relatively fertile water and moderate depth, while old iron-ore pits may attain depths of 500 to 600 feet or more. Shallow and moderate depth warm-water pits and quarries are usually stocked with bass or bluegills, although spring-fed pits may support stream trout.

Deep, cold iron mining pits can support stream trout and even lake trout populations, provided sufficient oxygen is maintained in the depths.

Man-Made Lakes

Also known as flowages, reservoirs or impoundments, man-made lakes are created by the damming of rivers. These dams can be formed on small or large rivers in either flat or steep lands, consequently creating smaller, shallower, or larger, deeper bodies of water, respectively; and like natural lakes, every man-made lake features its own unique set of qualities and characteristics.

Still, man-made lakes do share some similar characteristics. Since they follow a river channel, man-made lakes tend to be long and narrow. Current flow from the river flushes the water beneath the ice, good for supplying oxygen to winter fish; but increases or decreases in flow can fluctuate water levels, wreaking havoc with ice conditions and causing fish to move.

Like natural lakes, man-made lakes can be classified into groups based on geographic location, size, depth, shape, depth contours, water clarity and fertility. They're known as Canadian Shield, mountain, prairie and flatland reservoirs.

Canadian Shield reservoirs, as the name implies, are found on the infertile Canadian Shield and feature deep, rocky basins and cold water. They may feature cold-water species like lake trout in their

depths, and support cool-water fish like walleyes in shallower areas.

Mountain reservoirs are found in steep, hilly or mountainous regions of eastern and western North America, are narrow and feature moderately deep, steep-sided banks. With their moderately deep, steep breaking contours, rocky basins and cool to cold slightly fertile water, they support primarily stream trout, but may be suited to cool-water species like walleyes.

In contrast, prairie reservoirs of central Canada and the central United States are wider and feature warm, shallow, fertile water on the upper end and deep, cold, infertile water on the downstream end. Consequently, these reservoirs support good numbers of warm-water species such as largemouth bass and sunfish on the upper end and cool-water species like walleyes in the midsection, while maintaining populations of cold-water species such as salmon in the lower reaches.

Flatland reservoirs are surrounded by relatively flat geography and consequently cover wide, shallow expanses. Their shallow, bowl-shaped outlines and fertile waters support species such as largemouth bass, sunfish and white bass.

Big Rivers & Backwaters

BIG RIVERS

Due to their constant current flow, most river channels don't freeze solid enough to sustain ice-fishing opportunities, but in places where they do, winter fishing can be tremendous. Limited sections of rivers draining or feeding some Great Lakes bays, for example, often provide fabulous winter walleye, sauger and pike fishing, especially near late ice when the fish begin staging for their upstream spawning runs.

On large river systems such as the Mississippi (right), some large, deep, slow-flowing channels or eddies at the base of dams or locks allow limited windows of winter action for walleyes and saugers. Smaller, cold-water streams may even allow access to winter trout. Still, with flowing currents and fluctuating water levels, ice safety is at a premium, and ice conditions on flowing rivers must be monitored daily. You may find several inches of ice one day, only to find undercutting currents and fluctuating water flows have completely eroded the ice away the next day.

BACKWATERS

River backwaters in winter are simply frozen areas of slack water removed from the main current channel. They are usually large, encompassing vast expanses of surface area, and feature shallow, fertile, slow-moving water and sandy or silty bottoms covered with vegetation, or most commonly, flooded timber and stumps. Bordering the main channel you may find frozen, deeper secondary channels, sloughs or connecting lakes, which often feature more current flow than backwaters but less than the main channel.

Because most river backwaters are large in size, winter anglers enjoy exploring the distant, isolated edges of secluded backwater areas in the hopes of finding a private hotbed of ice-fishing action. And provided adequate water depth, cover, forage and oxygen are available, these adventurous ice fishermen are often successful. River backwater areas frequently attract many river species, including walleyes, pike, largemouth bass, white bass, yellow bass, crappies, perch and sunfish.

Ice-Fishing Equipment
& How to Use It

Winter Clothing

Anyone who has ever experienced a frigid northern winter knows the challenges of trying to stay warm and comfortable. At times, just walking between the driveway and house can be an experience some folks don't look forward to.

Few people understand the importance of staying warm and comfortable better than ice-fishing enthusiasts. Being subjected to continuous cold temperatures and brisk, icy winds pose constant challenges, even serious health threats, including frostbite, hypothermia and dehydration. But these things can be prevented by following a few simple precautions.

Begin by always being mindful of changing weather conditions, and if you start to feel cold, head for shore rather than risk a potentially hazardous situation. Most importantly, always prepare for each trip and dress wisely to avoid these serious situations in the first place.

Basic winter dressing strategies start with wearing multiple layers of clothing rather than a single, heavy layer, because multiple layers seal protective pockets of warm air between your body and icy outside temperatures. The inner tier should consist of light, comfortable, moisture-transferring material to keep you comfortable and dry, and the middle tiers should be light, yet bulky enough to trap pockets of warm air. The outside tier should be wind and water resistant to block frigid wind chills and keep moisture away from your warm, dry underclothing.

THE INNER TIER. A variety of quality, insulated synthetic underclothing is available under many brand names, but moisture-transferring polyester is the basis of any quality undergarment. Not only will polyester remain comfortable and warm, but because of its wicking properties, it also remains dry.

THE INSULATION TIER. Light, thick, low-density clothing materials such as wool or fleece make good insulation layers because they trap warm air pockets while accentuating the transfer of moisture away from the body.

THE OUTER TIER. The wind and water resistant tier should consist of Gore-Tex® lining that not only blocks the wind, but allows moisture to dissipate into the drier, colder, outside air. Two-piece outfits with numerous openings that can be zipped open during periods of activity or closed during periods of rest are especially good, because they allow you to either release excessive warmth or close it in as desired.

HATS & MITTS. Since most body heat is lost through the head, Polartec® pile insulated caps help ensure warmth by trapping body heat. Rag wool glomitts keep your hands warm on mild winter days, but for extreme temperatures you should wear bulky, polypropylene-lined mitts. Unlike gloves, which separate the fingers, mitts form a protective layer of warm air around the hands.

BOOTS & SOCKS. Today's heavily insulated pac boots are the choice of modern ice anglers. Some models feature waterproof Gore-Tex liners, which is a big advantage when there's water on the surface of the ice. Heavyweight wool socks worn next to the skin or over a polypropylene liner sock insure that your feet stay warm and dry.

ACCESSORIES. Ice Chaps™ (left) keep water from reaching your clothes when drilling holes.

Finally, pocket-size mitt and boot warmers are good to have along in case you find yourself getting cold. For more information on quality winter clothing, visit Cabela's® Inc. on the Internet at www.cabelas.com or call 1-800-237-4444.

Rods & Reels

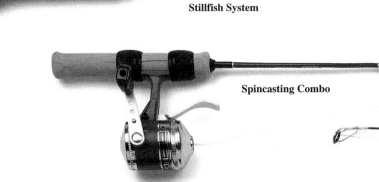

Jig Stick

Stillfish System

Spincasting Combo

Baitcasting Combo

Tremendous advancements in ice rod development have occurred in recent years. Compared to the past, the number of newly introduced styles, lengths, powers and actions being made available are coming in epidemic proportions.

Most modern ice anglers match these rods with high quality spinning reels—the type designed for ultra-light fishing during the open-water season. Correctly balanced, ice rod and reel combos not only make your fishing easier and more enjoyable, but also more successful.

ROD AND REEL TYPES

Ice-fishing rod and reel combos can be divided into the following seven categories:

JIG AND BOBBING STICKS can be as simple as a large, hand-held block of wood fashioned into a lineholder, or elaborate as wood- or plastic-handled fiberglass or graphite rod outfitted with a metal, wood or plastic linewinding device. Since these models don't feature a reel with drag, they're best used in shallow water with stronger than average lines for panfish. They're also the most reasonably priced rod option.

JIG POLES are wood-, plastic- or cork-handled fiberglass or graphite rods featuring a standard 1:1 gear ratio ice reel. Since these reels offer a simple drag, jig poles provide an economical option for anglers fishing shallow or mid-depth water for panfish.

STILLFISH SYSTEMS consist of a relatively stiff wood or cork handle and hollow graphite ice rods featuring a built-in stillfish reel. Instead of line being threaded through guides, line runs through the hollow blank. Unfortunately, stillfish reels feature low gear ratios and relatively poor drag systems.

ICE FLY SYSTEMS usually consist of sturdy, cork-handled graphite ice rods of varying lengths featuring a rear-positioned fly or spinning reel. The advantage is the rear-positioned reel allows the angler to keep their hand or finger on the line for exceptional lure control and fish-sensing feel.

SPINCASTING COMBOS are plastic, EVA foam or cork-handled fiberglass or graphite ice rods featuring a underspin-style spincast reel. Spincast combos cost more than standard jig poles, but the spincast reels they accommodate feature improved gear ratios and better drag systems, allowing ice anglers to fish deeper water and use lighter lines when pursuing panfish or medium-size gamefish.

SPINNING COMBOS are EVA foam or cork-handled fiberglass or graphite ice rods featuring a spinning reel. Quality spinning reels feature high gear ratios, sensitive, fine-tuned drag systems, and with the open spool line is less subject to freezing, making use of light lines possible. Depending on their size, spinning combos can be used for icing virtually any winter species from sunfish to salmon.

BAITCASTING COMBOS usually consist of stiff fiberglass or graphite ice rods of varying lengths and plastic, EVA foam or cork handles designed to accommodate a rounded, winch-like baitcast reel. Top-of-the-line baitcast reels feature high gear ratios, fine-tuned drag systems, large line capacity spools, and are usually used when fishing deep water or large fish such as pike, lake trout or salmon.

CHOOSING ICE RODS

As ice anglers take on the challenge of fishing multiple winter species, their collection of ice rods usually expands into dozens of models designed for more specialized ice-fishing purposes, based on the following qualities:

LENGTH. Long rods provide the most hook-setting power and fish-fighting control, but are limited to use outside a shanty. Short rods work better when fishing inside.

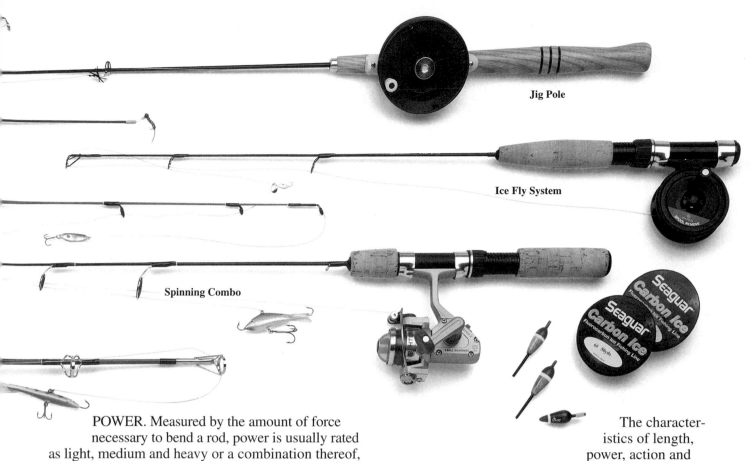

Jig Pole

Ice Fly System

Spinning Combo

POWER. Measured by the amount of force necessary to bend a rod, power is usually rated as light, medium and heavy or a combination thereof, such as medium heavy.

ACTION: Measured by where the rod bends, action is largely determined by the rod's taper. Action is rated as slow, medium, fast or a degree thereof, such as extra fast. A fast-action ice rod bends mainly at the tip, a medium-action bends at the midsection, and a slow-action bends over the rod's entire length.

SENSITIVITY: An ice rod's capability to detect light strikes is often called sensitivity. Typically, a fast-action graphite rod is the best way to achieve sensitivity.

The characteristics of length, power, action and sensitivity should be considered before purchasing an ice rod. For example, if you plan to fish for panfish, you'll want sensitive rods featuring light-power blanks, which allow use of ultralight lines and tiny lures while at the same time giving small fish the chance to put up a challenging fight. A good walleye rod, however, needs to have a fast action for precise jigging. And an effective northern pike or lake trout rod must be powerful enough to set the hook on a big, bony-mouthed fish and long enough to give you control during the fight.

Caring for Ice Rods and Reels

TRANSPORT rod and reel combos in a Ready Rig® Ice Professional carrying case. With an internal semi-rigid protective tube and cushioned lining, this case holds up to three ice-fishing combos completely assembled.

REMOVE a reel's thick grease and apply HT Blu-Lube to the gears for good cold weather performance.

Professional

Sweet Heart Plus

Finesse Plus

Thorne Brothers ice rods come in lengths and actions designed specifically for the modern ice angler. The "Professional" is available in both spinning and baitcasting models. These 32- to 42-inch rods can be built with graphite, solid-glass, or fiberglass-graphite composite blanks. Most anglers use the Professional for large walleyes, northern pike and lake trout. The "Sweet Pea," shown here with a Slater pole reel, is a 16-inch, solid-glass rod designed

Custom Ice-Fishing Rods

In the early 1980s, employees at Thorne Brothers Fishing Specialty Store in Fridley, Minn., began building high-quality ice rods in the store's custom rod shop. At the time, the modern ice-fishing revolution was just getting started with experts like Dave Genz experimenting with the use of sonar to find and catch winter fish. Dave quickly found that Thorne Brothers ice rods coupled with ultralight spinning reels and light lines were the perfect match for the precise lure presentations needed to get finicky winter fish to bite.

The first ice rods to come from the custom shop were made from fly rod tip sections purchased from some of the major fly rod manufacturers. The tip sections arrived to the shop as "blanks," meaning no guides were attached. After sorting the blanks into light, medium and heavy actions, Thorne Brothers rod builders went to work and fitted the blanks with small cork handles, guides and tip tops. Finally, tightly wound electrical tape

Custom rod builder gluing on a tip top

was used to hold small spinning reels securely in place, thereby eliminating the need for cold-to-the-touch metal reel seats.

Today, the store's best-selling ice rods are made from incredibly sensitive and durable solid-graphite or solid-fiberglass rod blanks, all of which are designed by the Thorne Brothers staff. These blanks are manufactured to exacting specifications for the sole purpose of catching more fish through the ice. Like in the early days, the blanks are built into a finished ice rod by hand, one at a time. Regardless of whether you need a 16-inch sight-fishing rod for big bluegills (p. 62), or a 32-inch "Dead Stick" for finicky walleyes (p. 79), Thorne Brothers builds a rod to suit your needs.

If you'd like to order one of the best ice rods money can buy, contact Thorne Brothers by phone at 612-572-3782, or check them out on the Internet at www.fishandgame.com/thornebros

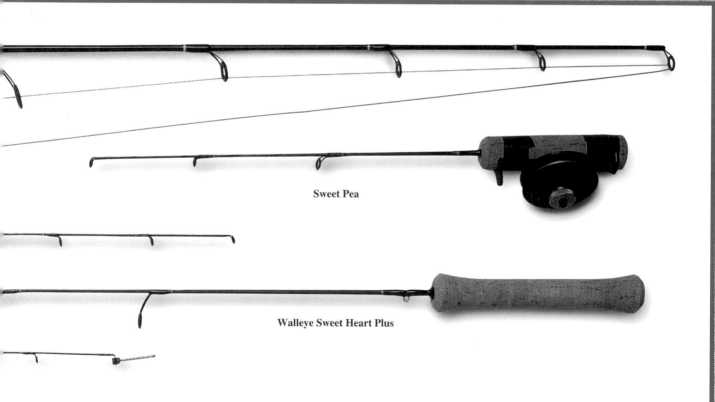

Sweet Pea

Walleye Sweet Heart Plus

for sight fishing in shallow, clear water. The "Sweet Heart Plus" is the most popular panfish rod in the Thorne Brothers line. These 24- to 28-inch solid-graphite rods are tremendously sensitive. The "Walleye Sweet Heart Plus" is available in medium or medium-heavy actions. Many ice experts think this 28-inch solid-graphite rod is the finest walleye jigging rod on the market today. The "Finesse Plus" is a 19-inch solid-graphite rod, which is short enough for sight fishing, yet long enough for fishing with sonar. The custom-made built-in spring bobber, an optional item for this rod, telegraphs the lightest panfish bites.

Lines & Knots

The surge of interest in winter fishing has brought numerous advancements in specialty lines, each specifically suited to special ice-fishing conditions.

LINE TYPES

BRAIDED DACRON LINES rated from 15- to 60-pound test are commonly used as tip-up backing. Vinyl- or teflon-coated versions are designed to not soak up water, making them more resistant to freezing. While vinyl-coated dacron tends to have a great deal of memory, teflon-coated lines remain flexible even in the coldest temperatures.

STANDARD MONOFILAMENTS are used on linewinders, plastic ice reels, spincast, spinning or baitcast reels in varying break strengths. They may also be used for tip-up leader material. Thin, flexible, clear or green monofilaments are the choice of most ice anglers, although some anglers like fluorescent lines for greater visibility or "cold weather" designations, which are usually blue in color and specially formulated for winter usage.

MICRO MONO, or very thin diameter monofilaments commonly rated under 2 pound break strengths, are used for presenting micro-sized lures to panfish. Some innovative anglers even use transparent nylon sewing thread, often called "invisible thread," on their ultralight spinning reels. As a bonus, invisible thread is inexpensive; most fabric stores sell 100-yard spools of it for about a dollar.

"SUPERLINES," which are made of Kevlar®, Spectra® or MicroDyneema® material, feature little stretch and a very thin diameter for their break-strength, often offering twice as much or more strength for their diameter than comparably rated monofilaments. They're used mostly for deep-water jigging. Because some superlines are easy for fish to see in clear water, many anglers use 3- to 4-foot fluorocarbon leaders. When fluorocarbon is immersed in water, it blends in so well it's almost invisible.

WIRE LINES come in single-strand and braided varieties. Multi-strand are used mainly for deep-water jigging because of their no-stretch properties, but if not properly cared for, they easily kink. Both single and braided wire lines are also used to make wire leaders and rigs for tip-up fishing.

KNOTS

It's well documented that knots weaken line, but some fare better than others. Below are three quality, easy-to-tie knots commonly used in ice fishing that retain close to 100% of the line's originally rated tensile strength.

Duncan Loop, Strength 90%

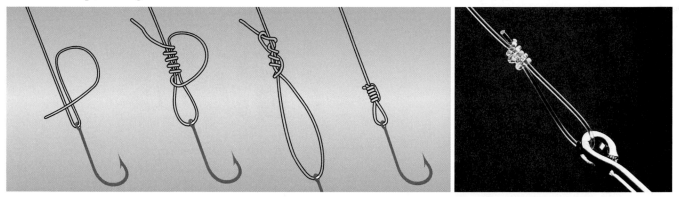

SLIDE your line through the hook eye, and form a loop in the tag end as shown. Pass the tag end through the loop, winding around the standing line and top section of the loop four or five times while moving away from the hook. Moisten the line and pull the tag end to tighten the knot. Slide the knot to the desired position by pulling on the standing line, and trim the tag end.

Trilene Knot, Strength 90%

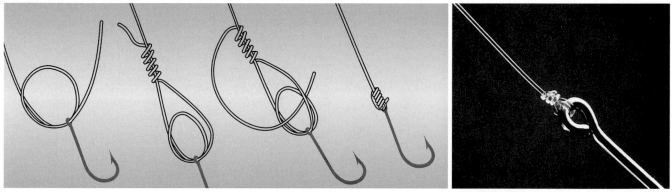

SLIDE your line through the hook eye, and repeat, entering the line from the same direction and being sure to form a double loop at the hook eye, as shown. Wrap the tag end around the standing line four or five times, moving away from the hook. Pass the tag end back through the double loop at the hook eye, moisten, pull the knot tight against the hook eye and trim tag.

Palomar Knot, Strength 95%

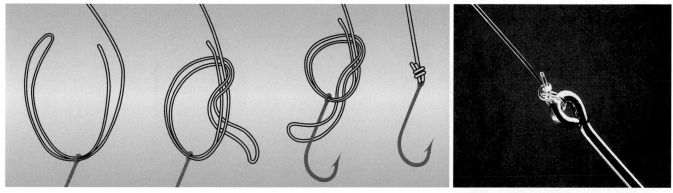

PASS your line through the hook eye, and return it through in the opposite direction to form a long loop, as shown. Bring the loop back over the doubled line and tie an overhand knot around the hook eye. Place the loop over the hook or lure and pull the standing line to draw the knot tight around the hook eye. Tighten and trim tag.

Tip-Ups & Rattle Reels

While some ice-fishing anglers use only rods and reels, the vast majority make tip-ups and rattle reels an important part of their arsenal. In fact, some ice-fishing enthusiasts prefer watching the flag fly on a tip-up or hear the bells ring on a rattle reel over feeling a fish strike on an ice rod.

TIP-UPS

Catching fish with tip-ups is a deep-rooted ice-fishing tradition, dating back many years. In fact, it's been speculated that tip-ups of some form may have been used by early Native Americans using ice fishing as a means of sustenance which, if true, would make tip-ups one of the earliest forms of ice tackle.

The basic concept behind the term "tip-up" is simply a device consisting of a body supporting a reel of line. Attached to the reel is a loaded trip mechanism that causes a signal to flip upright when a fish strikes. Early models are thought to have consisted of a tapered branch frozen into surface snow, a length of gut string and a baited bone or claw hook. The gut string could be tied to the branch tip with a fore-length of backing and the opposite, baited end lowered into the hole; strikes could be detected when the branch jiggled up and down.

Today, tip-ups are used as a means of recreation, and many technological advances have made them

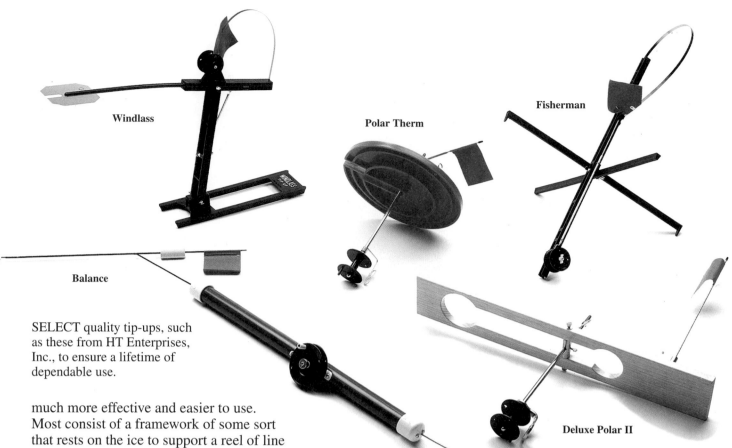

Windlass

Polar Therm

Fisherman

Balance

Deluxe Polar II

SELECT quality tip-ups, such as these from HT Enterprises, Inc., to ensure a lifetime of dependable use.

much more effective and easier to use. Most consist of a framework of some sort that rests on the ice to support a reel of line and a spring-loaded trip mechanism that flips up a flag when the reel is turned by a biting fish. To prevent the reel, line and flag mechanism from freezing, most quality designs now feature underwater reels and sealed, lubricated trip mechanisms. While many tip-up anglers spool with dacron backing, the experts prefer nylon or teflon-coated dacron which don't soak up water and help prevent freezing. Fish are caught by pulling on the line to set the hook, then hand over handing the fish to the surface.

As various innovations have spawned new ideas over the generations, different tip-up models have appeared, offering various features such as multiple reel sizes, freeze-proof trips, built-in hole covers, reel drag and adjustable tension settings, but all can be grouped into seven basic classifications:

BASIC CROSS MEMBER TIP-UPS consist of two interlocking, horizontal bars supporting a centerpiece. The centerpiece has an underwater reel filled with dacron line and a leader tipped with a baited hook tied at the end. The centerpiece and reel are placed in the water to prevent the reel and line from freezing, and a greased wire trip mechanism leading from the reel to the flag is angled so when a fish strikes and the reel spins, the wire turns, releasing a spring-loaded flag, indicating the strike to anglers. While cross member designs are typically the most economical, the release mechanisms are seldom sealed, they're prone to freeze up, and there is no way to adjust reel tension on most models.

UNDERWATER TIP-UPS consist of a rectangular, horizontal body supporting a centerpiece. Like the cross member tip-up, this centerpiece features an underwater reel—but the reel is directly connected to a shaft leading to a flag trip mechanism, so when the reel turns and line is peeled off, the flag is released to indicate a strike. On high quality models, the shaft is placed within a sealed, lubricated cylinder that is unlikely to freeze, and the frames are "V" shaped to prevent freeze-down. Trip tension can be increased or decreased by setting the flag on the heavy or light trips, or on high quality models, adjusting the spindle mechanism to increase the angle of the flag wire against the trip. The one disadvantage to rectangular underwater tip-ups is that the frame allows light and snow to enter hole around the centerpiece, and leaves the hole around the trip cylinder subject to freezing.

THERMAL TIP-UPS consist of a flat horizontal body that supports a centerpiece and completely covers your hole, thereby blocking light and snow from entering the hole and resisting hole freeze-up. With the large, wide bodies of these models, however-er, transportation on the ice is often bulky.

WIND TIP-UPS consist of a tall, upright body supporting a movable arm outfitted with a reel of dacron line, leader and a baited hook or lure on one end, and a large, flat plate on the other. The line extends from the reel through a hole in this plate and down into the water. A strip of spring steel is bent over to the reel from the end the arm, so when the reel turns, the flag trips up, indicating the strike.

A spring-loaded tension bracket leading from the center body to the reel end of the arm allows tension on the arm to be made lighter for smaller baits, and stronger for larger ones. The same bracket also allows the arm to be directed higher to achieve a wider, more aggressive jigging motion, or lower to create less movement. While the jigging motion keeps your bait moving, which can increase your productivity, these tip-ups only function during warm winter days when the hole and exposed reel aren't subject to freeze up.

MAGNETIC TIP-UPS feature a hollow centerpiece with an internal spring-loaded flag shaft, all supported by a tripod. The bottom portion of the centerpiece holds the underwater reel. A magnet on the reel and another just opposite the reel at the base of the internal spring-loaded flag mechanism are aligned to hold the reel in place by magnetic tension. When a fish bites and the reel turns, this magnetic tension is broken, allowing the flag to release and indicates the strike to an angler. Reel tension can be adjusted by raising or lowering the reel, thereby increasing or decreasing the magnetic force between the magnets.

TIP-DOWNS AND BALANCE TIP-UPS feature an upright body style much like a wind tip-up, but the body supports either a fulcrum-balanced jig stick, rod and reel, or movable rod. With a jig rod or rod and reel, the rod simply "tips down" off balance

when a fish strikes, and left in free spool, line is fed to the fish until the angler arrives to set the hook. The rod can then be removed and the fish fought freely with the rod and reel. On movable rod designs, line simply runs through a wire loop at the arm's tip, and down to a free-spooled rattle reel attached to the side of the body. When a fish strikes, the arm tips down and the spool feeds line. Tension can be controlled using the reel's drag.

POPULAR TIP-UP RIGS. Standard tip-up riggings consist of a barrel or ball-bearing swivel connecting the dacron backing to a monofilament, Spectra—or in the case of fishing toothy species like pike or pickerel—wire, leader. A baited (usually a live minnow) single or treble hook weighted with an appropriate number of split shot to lower and hold the bait at the desired depth rounds out the rig.

At times, it pays to add painted hooks, metal or plastic spinners, spoons, flashers or other attractors to draw fish. With moving, wind-style tip-ups, some innovative winter anglers have even begun using colorful jigs or small flutter spoons to increase their attractive qualities.

At the end of the day, attach tip-up line holders (right) to the tip-up spools to prevent the line from unraveling and becoming tangled during storage and transport.

How to Use an Underwater Tip-Up

SET the flag arm under the T-shaped spindle after lowering your bait to the desired depth (left). For walleye fishing, set the arm under the smooth side of the spindle so it will trip easily. Set the arm under the grooved side for northern pike fishing with large minnows. A bite is signalled by a tripped flag (center). You can tell how fast a fish is moving with your bait by how fast the spindle is turning (inset). If the spindle isn't turning, gently pull on the line until you feel resistance. Set the hook with a sharp snap of your wrist (right).

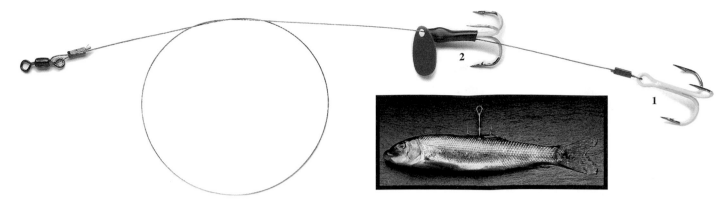

USE a single treble hook (inset) or a quick-strike rig when fishing large minnows. On a quick-strike rig, place the end treble (1) through the top of the minnow behind the head, then hook the second treble (2) near the minnow's dorsal fin. These rigs allow anglers to set the hook immediately upon a strike thereby reducing the chances of deeply hooked fish.

RATTLE REELS

In large permanent houses, those equipped with beds for sleeping, anglers often use rattle reels to keep lines in the water throughout the entire night. In fact, few things in winter angling are as exciting as waking to the sound of a spinning rattle reel.

Most models are simple free-spooling plastic (right) or wood spools featuring an internal or external rattle that makes noise when they turn as a fish strikes, alerting anglers to a bite. They are usually fastened to the walls of a ice shanty, but can also be attached to a bucket or stand for outside use. When used outside, however, rattle reels are subject to freeze up much like wind tip-ups.

Anglers usually load the spool of the rattle reel with dacron line, a fixed bobber, and a live- or dead-bait rig identical to the type used for tip-up fishing. The

best rattle reels feature adjustable spool tension knobs that can be set light enough so a fish doesn't feel any resistance as it takes line, but tight enough so as to not get a backlash if a fish makes a hard initial run and then stops abruptly.

The best method to play and land a fish hooked on a rattle reel system is for one angler to fight the fish and take in line by hand while a second angler simultaneously winds in the slack line onto the rattle reel. This way, the line doesn't become entangled and resetting the bait is easy.

How to Use a Wind Tip-Up

BEND the metal plate upward so it catches more wind if you want the bait to bob more intensely (left). The tension of the coil spring (arrow) also regulates the action. Loosen the wing nut, then slide the spring downward for more action; slide it upward for less action. Set the flag by bending the thin metal flag spring so that it presses against the back side of the spool (center). Pressure from the spring prevents the spool from turning and fixes the depth. When a fish bites, friction from the turning spool springs the flag (right).

Lures & Terminal Tackle

Like serious open water anglers, die-hard winter fishing enthusiasts have realized fish eat a variety of food items beneath the ice. They understand the importance of learning to use a variety of different lure styles, and carrying each design in several sizes, shapes and colors, enabling them to meticulously adjust their tactics depending on the target species' environment, type of forage and activity level. And like open-water fishing, lures must be matched with the appropriate terminal tackle to perform to their full potential.

LURES

Ice-fishing lures come in virtually every style, shape, size and color imaginable, so it's easy to understand why many beginning anglers may be confused by what they see. However,

for simplicity, ice lures can be grouped into seven basic categories: teardrops, ice flies, plastics, jigging minnows, spoons, swimming jigs and bladebaits.

TEARDROPS are essentially small bits of lead or metal molded or soldered to a hook. Designed to represent various zooplankton and insect larvae, they come in an almost infinite variety of sizes, styles and colors. Naturally sized and colored teardrops work best in clear water. In dark or colored water, ice fishermen should use larger, flashier and more colorful teardrops to get the fish's attention.

ICE FLIES, basically modified teardrop ice jigs featuring rubber, plastic or hair dressings, come in a vari-

Teardrops

Ice Flies

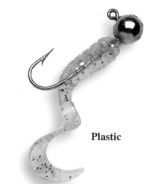

Plastic

ety of sizes and styles and are designed to represent mostly zooplankton or insect larvae. Used primarily for panfish, naturally sized and colored flies work best in clear water, while larger, more colorful or flashier patterns are better in dark or colored water.

PLASTICS can consist of anything from ultra-thin, vibrating strips to large tube or twist-tail style lures. Since they have a natural, soft texture and feel and are worked slowly, they work best in clear water when trying to tempt light-biting, fussy fish. They may be added to various jig heads or spoons, but can be fished on plain hooks.

JIGGING MINNOWS are gliding lures that when lifted and dropped abruptly, dart to the side. They represent darting minnows, work well in clear or dark water, and are good bets when trying to cover water, work aggressive fish or trigger finicky biters.

SPOONS are long, narrow or wide-bodied metal lures, usually featuring shiny nickel, gold or copper finishes that may be accented with glitter, prism tape, beads or paint to help attract fish. When jigged, they dart, flutter and flash to represent struggling, dying bait-fish. Spoons are effective for attracting fish in deep or dark water, working semi-aggressive fish or for triggering finicky fish.

SWIMMING JIGS are gliding lures that when lifted and dropped glide in a circular motion, representing dying baitfish. They're effective when trying to cover water, and work well in clear or dark water when trying to tempt aggressive fish or trigger finicky fish.

BLADEBAITS are thin, narrow, forward-weighted slices of plated or painted metal that when aggressively pulled upward, wiggle with an intense, tight fish-attracting wiggle. They're great for working dark water, active and aggressive fish, or triggering strikes from neutral fish.

Winter anglers usually sweeten ice lures with grubs, maggots, minnows or bits of live bait. Those skillfully fishing a versatile array of these lures set with vari-ous innovative riggings and jigging cadences are often among the most consistently successful anglers on the ice.

TERMINAL TACKLE

In addition to carrying a good assortment of lures, successful ice fishermen carry a wide variety of terminal tackle. The most important items include the following:

BOBBERS AND FLOATS. Small sponge, Styrofoam® or balsa ice floats are usually pegged or clipped to the line. Some can be rigged as slip-floats, which allow line to slide through the float body up to a small bobber stop, allowing rod-and-reel anglers to retrieve fish from deep water without removing the float. Sponge floats are popular with some anglers because ice buildup can easily be squeezed off.

SPRING BOBBERS. Sensitive spring bobbers clip or adhere to rod tips. The fishing line runs through the spring at the rod tip, allowing anglers to detect even the slightest strikes.

SINKERS. From micro-shot used to precisely weight tiny bobbers to large Rubber-cor® weights for keeping large minnows in place on tip-ups, sinkers are a must for many ice-fishing situations.

SNAPS. Small snaps allow anglers to quickly change jigging spoons without retying.

HOOKS. Depending on the winter species being targeted, hook sizes range from tiny #14's for finicky sunfish to large 4/0's for lake trout and pike.

LEADERS. Lure or bait rigs for toothy fish like northern pike require some type of wire leader to prevent bite-offs. Mono leaders are often attached to dacron tip-up or rattle reel lines for walleyes and other wary species.

SWIVELS. Many ice fishermen use swivels to attach mono leaders to the main line when rigging tip-ups and rattle reels.

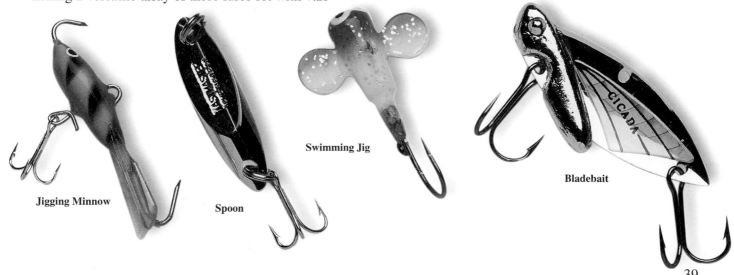

Jigging Minnow

Spoon

Swimming Jig

Bladebait

Shelters

ost modern ice anglers use some type of shelter to keep warm. Ice shelters, also called houses, shacks, shanties or huts, vary from portable canvas windbreaks to elaborate, carpeted cabins with all the amenities of home. While a number of different shelter styles and sizes have appeared on the market, each model basically falls into one of five distinct categories: windbreak, collapsible, mobile, portable or permanent.

WINDBREAKS are simply two- or three-sided structures that can be positioned to block the wind. They're usually lightweight, easy to transport and work well for the mobile angler, but don't provide full protection in super cold weather, and most are limited to protection for only one person.

The best windbreaks feature a place to sit and provide enough room to store your equipment out of freezing winds, yet set up and break down easily and compactly for convenient transport and storage.

COLLAPSIBLE SHELTERS (below) are lightweight, self-contained units that are easy to transport, easy to set up in calm weather and provide full protection. They work especially well when hiking or snowshoeing to remote waters, but are difficult to set up in stiff winter winds. They're available in vari-

ous sizes, but usually accommodate no more than two anglers comfortably.

Top-of-the-line collapsible models feature ample room and hole positioning capabilities, and are constructed with a sturdy framework and draped windows, which are a nice feature, as they allow you to see out and either let light in or close it out as desired.

Many anglers have had the unfortunate experience of stepping out of their collapsible shelters for a moment, only to watch the wind glide the shanty across the ice into the frozen distance. Ice anchors (right) are a handy option for just such situations, as they allow a means of stabilizing these shelters.

To insert an ice anchor, gently tap the base in, and begin twisting while firmly applying pressure to the top of the anchor until the threads grip and begin turning down. Some anglers also tie guidelines from anchors to shelter walls to help prevent the sides from bowing in heavy winds.

MOBILE SHELTERS are self-contained units slightly heavier than windbreaks or collapsibles. They are simple to set up and break down, provide full protection, and with sled bases offer a convenient means of storing and transporting gear. They're available in both one- and two-man designations.

Quality mobile models offer a comfortable seat or platform, a large and deep enough sled base to adequately hold and transport your gear, and ample room to fish with the top down. Some models feature variable top positions, allowing you to set the roof vertically to create a windbreak, or part way down to allow ventilation while using a portable heater. The most famous mobile shelter ever manufactured, the Fish

Trap (above), continues to be the shelter of choice among North America's top ice experts.

PORTABLE SHELTERS (below) typically feature a plastic or wood floor, and an aluminum or steel frame surrounded by canvas, polyethylene or nylon material. Depending on size, they become increasingly heavy and difficult to pull, transport and store, but are relatively easy to set up, provide full protection, and folded down allow a means of transporting gear. They're also available in a variety of sizes to accommodate various numbers of anglers.

The best portable models are easy to set up, allow standing room, and feature two wide opening, zippered doors and plenty of space for holes to accommodate the number of people you plan to fish with. In addition, quality portables have a sturdy frame and tightly sewn, quiet overlaid material, yet are lightweight for easy pulling or towing.

PERMANENT SHELTERS (below) are usually large, wood- or aluminum-framed structures, often featuring storm doors, windows and stoves, even multiple rooms with beds or a second story. Properly trailered or rigged with drop hitches they can be moved, but because they're so heavy and transport is time-consuming, they're not considered portable.

CHOOSING A SHELTER. The key to choosing the shelter style that best suits your needs can be determined by the way you fish. If you plan to set up in one spot, permanent shelters are hard to beat, as they're roomy, comfortable and warm, but you will need a means of transporting the unit and a place to store it off-season. Portable and collapsible models work well if you plan to move only once or twice in a day of fishing, but if you want to fish lots of holes and stay on active fish, most experts agree that mobile shelters are the best choice.

Augers & Chisels

Every ice-fishing adventure begins with chopping or cutting holes. Once a dreaded chore, the recent movement toward mobility in ice fishing has brought much-needed advancements in ice-cutting technology. Many ice pros figuratively refer to drilling holes and moving to find active fish as "casting through the ice."

Holes can be chopped with a bladed chisel to the desired size, or cut with hand or power ice drills to form holes of specific diameters, usually ranging from 4 to 10 inches. Your choice should be based on ice thickness, the species you're targeting and their expected size. Many veteran ice anglers use the smallest diameter hole they can get away with for two reasons: 1) small holes are easier to cut than large holes, which makes moving to find active fish easier; 2) fish can't turn around and keep fighting once they enter a small hole, which reduces the number of fish lost "in the hole."

CHISELS

STANDARD CHISELS, or spuds, are a long-handled metal blade, flattened on one side and angled along the other to form a thin, sharp point. Simple and economical, standard chisels work well for testing ice thickness, but are noisy, often spook fish, and make chopping holes difficult when ice is thick.

DELUXE CHISELS, such as the Jiffy® Mille Lacs Ice Chisel (above) feature weighted handles for increasing chopping

Jiffy Legend Lightning gas auger

power, and specialized cutting surfaces to increase cutting depth with each chop. Their special stepped edges allow precise chopping, and can be used to flare out the bottom of holes or shave ice. Some models also feature pinned, height adjustable handles.

HAND AUGERS

Well-sharpened hand augers are reasonably priced, light-weight, and therefore the choice of many anglers. However, they can be taxing to use when ice gets thick.

STANDARD HAND AUGERS, such as the StrikeMaster® Mora (left), are the most economical choice, but the blades must be regularly replaced to maintain peak cutting efficiency.

MODERN HAND AUGER designs, such as the StrikeMaster Lazer, feature a special set of angled blades (right) that not only reduce the amount of time necessary between blade replacements, but make hole cutting easier and faster. Some models feature off-set handles, which may take awhile to master, but allow two-handed turning power, greatly increasing the auger's cutting speed.

POWER AUGERS

Extremely popular among today's ice angler, power augers feature a drill assembly with a motorized powerhead to turn the auger at a controlled rate.

ELECTRIC AUGERS (below) feature electric powerheads that run on 12-volt batteries. Due to the lack of fumes produced by electric augers, they're popular with people drilling holes in enclosed shanties.

GAS AUGERS (opposite page) feature gas powerheads generally ranging from 2- to 3½-horsepower motors and gear boxes of varying ratios. They

Big Holes for Big Fish

The Ice Angler™ is a cutting device that attaches to a gas auger drill and automatically enlarges the base of your hole into a conical shape as you pull up on the auger. The wide-based hole helps anglers slip large fish into the hole with ease.

are the choice of most serious ice anglers, as they cut through ice of any thickness efficiently, are easy to use and don't require lugging along heavy batteries to operate. The drawback is they're relatively bulky and heavy, and more difficult to transport on the ice. Some manufacturers even make muffler exhaust kits for their gas augers that allow you to drill shanty holes without fumes.

Some versatile ice anglers carry interchangeable power auger drill assemblies of varying diameter so they're ready for multiple situations. And in mid-winter, when the ice gets very thick, anglers install auger extensions that lengthen the drill assembly by 6 to 12 inches.

Regardless of whether you use an electric, gas or hand auger, you should coat the blades with a layer of household oil or petroleum jelly to prevent rusting. Even a small amount of rust can greatly reduce a blade's cutting capability.

StrikeMaster Electra Lazer

43

Sonar Devices

Historically, ice anglers depended on clip-on lead weights to determine depth. By drilling hole after hole, anglers could drop these weights to bottom, repeatedly measure depths and eventually locate drop-offs and other underwater structures. Those with a sensitive touch could even differentiate hard bottom from soft bottom. But this was a time-consuming, often difficult task.

Today, modern sonar makes the same process relatively easy. These sensitive electronic devices feature transmitter/receivers called transducers that transmit sound waves to the bottom, receive these echos back after they bounce off bottom and return, then display these signals on a dial or screen. Once ice anglers learn to understand these displays they can easily determine depth, and by simply moving through an area and noting the depth at various points, piece together the precise location of drop-offs, underwater points, humps, holes, weeds, timber, rocks, plankton, baitfish, gamefish and differentiate bottom hardness.

The sonar available to the modern ice angler is nothing short of amazing. In fact, many anglers don't even drill holes through the ice unless they first spot gamefish with their sonar. How is that possible? By simply pouring water on solid, clear ice and placing the transducer in the water, the unit can transmit

Dave Genz using his sonar to find and catch perch, sunfish and crappies

Zercom LCF-40 Ice

Vexilar FL-8SLT

Zercom ColorPoint

and receive sound waves through the ice, allowing you to see the depth, weeds and even fish.

SONAR TYPES

Sonar comes in a variety of types, but traditional flashers, liquid crystal flashers, liquid crystal graphs (LCG's) and some hand-held specialty models are the primary tools of modern ice anglers.

TRADITIONAL FLASHERS, such as the Vexilar® FL-8SLT and Zercom® ColorPoint, show the sonar signal on a calibrated dial, which reveals depth, bottom content, cover, fish, even your lure or bait. Uniquely, flashers provide a simultaneous reaction display. In other words, if you move your lure, you see its motion displayed on the screen at the same time, providing a distinct advantage for ice anglers who want to see when fish are moving in and how they're reacting to precise presentations. Traditional flashers do, however, require a great deal of battery "juice" to power a motor and bulb, making it necessary to recharge batteries after a few days of hard use.

LIQUID CRYSTAL FLASHERS. Like traditional flashers, liquid crystal flashers display the sonar signal on a calibrated dial display and, due to some spectacular engineering feats, provide simultaneous reaction display. Some models, like the Zercom

LCF-40 Ice, are custom-designed for ice fishing and feature special grade freeze-resistant display fluids. Liquid crystal flashers use much less battery juice than traditional flashers, extending battery life.

LIQUID CRYSTAL GRAPHS. LCG's display the sonar signal on a televisionlike screen made up of varying numbers of squares, called *pixels*, which reveal depth, bottom content, cover, fish and your lure or bait. The larger the number of pixels, the more defined the resulting picture. While close, response time is not simultaneous as it is with traditional flashers—a disadvantage when immediate response times are desired. Liquid crystal graphs also feature liquid filled screens, making them subject to freeze up if a cold-weather grade liquid is not used.

SPECIALTY SONAR. Gun- or hand-held units, such as the StrikeMaster Polar Vision (right), are a convenient way of determining depth and the presence of fish, but aren't as useful for providing information regarding bottom hardness and presence of cover.

IMPORTANT SONAR FEATURES

Once you've chosen the sonar style that best meets your ice-fishing needs, you'll want to consider several important features when selecting a specific unit, including portability, depth capability, transducer style and angle, power, frequency, target separation and display resolution.

PORTABILITY is crucial, because you'll need to easily carry the unit from hole to hole to locate and catch active fish. Most sonar devices marketed for the ice fisherman include either a durable plastic case or zippered carrying case (left).

DEPTH CAPABILITY is the unit's ability to display signals from shallow or deep water. Most units feature several ranges, such as 0-30, 0-60, 0-120 and 0-240, and a number of modern LCG units even allow you to program the specific depth range being covered, allowing you to "zoom" in on a specific range or feature you want to view in greater detail.

Battery Basics

Most ice anglers have declared gel-cell batteries the winter sonar battery of choice. They're relatively lightweight, won't leak acid and can be drained and recharged numerous times without needing replacing. For best results, bring your battery inside after each use, and once the battery reaches room temperature, charge overnight to maintain the battery at peak charge. Batteries should also be charged periodically during long-term storage.

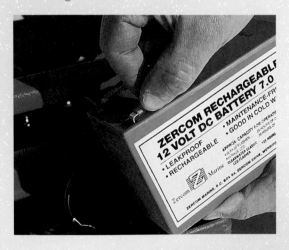

FLASHER COLOR is a flasher readout dial presented in color. The Vexilar FL-8SLT, for example, shows the strongest signals in bright red, light signals in green, and modest signals in orange, making it a very user-friendly flasher.

A TRANSDUCER is the sonar device's transmitter and receiver. The primary consideration here is the unit's cone angle, which determines how large of a cone-shaped area the sonar sound waves cover. A narrow cone angle concentrates the signal strength into a small area, making it best for detecting fish holding in deep water or tight to bottom. A wide cone angle spreads the signal throughout a larger area, making it weaker, but good for covering more water, detecting suspended fish or locating fish in shallow water. Some units may feature a dual or three-way transducer, which allows you to interchange between two or more cone angles.

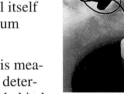

A SELF-ALIGNING TRANSDUCER is a big advantage to ice anglers, simply because the transducer is suspended in the water, causing it to automatically level itself and provide optimum readings.

SONAR POWER is measured in watts and determines the strength behind the sound waves being distributed to the bottom. The more power a unit has, the more potential it has for obtaining detailed readings, including small targets in deep water. Most units run 400 to 1000 watts of power.

FREQUENCY is measured in kilohertz (kHz) and simply determines the pattern of the sound waves being distributed and received by the transducer. Most units feature 200 kHz. The advantage of using a different frequency is simply that interference from other units is decreased or eliminated.

TARGET SEPARATION is the distance a transducer receiver and display screen or dial can separate targets appearing within the sonar cone. The smaller the target separation, the more clear your readings will be.

DISPLAY RESOLUTION is the ability of a calibrated dial to display the details of a signal being provided by the transducer. A liquid crystal graph with a powerful transducer and low pixel count, for example, may pick up detailed signals but not be able to fully display them.

HOW TO USE SONAR

Often, the biggest difference between the catch of an ice-fishing expert and everyday angler is the expert's knowledgeable use of sonar. By learning how to properly read what the unit is revealing and taking advantage of that knowledge, experts vastly improve their understanding of the under-ice environment and how fish are reacting to it, then make the adjustments necessary to increase their winter catches.

To set up a flasher-type sonar for ice fishing, be sure the power button is in the "off" position, then connect your power and transducer cords to the unit, and hook up the battery. Next, set your transducer level in the hole, turn on the unit, and lower your lure about 5 feet down. Increase the gain until you clearly see the bottom and just make out your jig. Fish will now show up as they move through the sonar signal. Note that as you lower your jig deeper, you may need to turn up the gain with some units to ensure good readings.

As you spend time viewing your flasher screen, look for the following signals:

DEPTH AND BOTTOM CONTENT. Depth appears as a solid band. On the Vexilar FL-8SLT shown below, the depth is 14 feet. Rock, gravel or sand bottoms are indicated by a second mark (double echo) at exactly twice the real depth; soft bottoms, by a wide, dim band, with no second mark.

A LURE appears as a distinct, solid mark suspended at the depth you've lowered it. The gain on a Vexilar should be adjusted so the lure shows as a green or green/orange mark.

BAITFISH AND PLANKTON appear as thin marks unconnected to bottom. The Vexilar shows baitfish as thin, green marks. Because baitfish are often moving quickly, their flasher signal quivers and moves accordingly.

WEEDS AND OTHER COVER appear as irregular, thin, stationary marks projecting off bottom. On the Vexilar, weeds show up as thin, green marks.

FISH appear as distinct, strong, solid marks either suspended or holding just off bottom. The Vexilar indicates a fish located directly below the hole as a bright red mark.

Underwater Cameras

The introduction of sophisticated electronic equipment such as sonar has changed the way ice anglers fish by displaying depth and indicating the presence of various sub-ice features. Underwater cameras now pick up where sonar left off, not only by indicating what's below, but by providing an actual visual picture of what's below the ice, presented on a television monitor.

Underwater cameras are essentially a specially weighted, stabilized lens suspended on a flexible co-axial cable placed in a cold-resistant urethane housing. A standard television jack on the opposite cable end accommodates a small black-and-white television monitor. Usually operated as 12-volt systems, specialized lenses and plug ends now available also allow these cameras to be hooked up to color television monitors, or directly to camcorders for taping and subsequent viewing. Some units even attach to a

wearable, face-mask-like shield and headset system that display the images from below directly onto a three-dimensional, virtual reality style display screen.

To use underwater cameras, a hole to accommodate the camera lens is drilled a few feet away from where an angler is fishing (above). In clear water, the lens's range is approximately 2½ times the distance you can see down, but most camera

holes are 4 to 6 feet away from the actual fishing hole. A large lure or easily visible object is then lowered down the fishing hole, and the cable is turned until the target object appears on the screen. You're then ready to begin fishing.

However, unless you have an infrared model, underwater cameras have limited potential during twilight and evening periods or in dark water, as artificially produced light tends to provide poor results. Television monitors may also be difficult to view in bright light, and should be shielded from glare. The most popular underwater

camera on the market, the Nature Vision Aqua-Vu, features a monitor set deep inside a built-in sun shield.

THE CAMERA CATCH. On the positive side, underwater cameras provide an enlightening, richer appreciation for fish in their under-ice environment while allowing ice anglers to positively identify under-ice features and fish species. The downside is many ice anglers using cameras admit that they easily become distracted, often spending more time watching the monitor than actually fishing. Another camera concern may be the identification of tightly grouped, seldom-moving fish that can be subject to overharvest by the irresponsible.

Maps & Navigation Equipment

Lake and reservoir maps allow you to identify depth contours, potential fish-holding features and the closest public access points to them. Many lake maps include additional important symbols depicting bottom content, weeds, timber, river channels, dams and inlets. Other valuable information, such as a listing of primary forage and fish species present, may also be included.

Some specialized maps furnish latitude and longitude markings and coordinates as well, allowing you to efficiently use them in conjunction with another electronic tool available to serious ice anglers: navigation equipment. The most commonly employed navigation system is a Global Positioning System (GPS). Essentially, GPS elec-

tronically determines your precise global coordinates, along with other significant programmed locations referred to as *waypoints*.

Waypoints may include coordinates for your access site and specific, potential fish-holding features. By entering and saving these specific waypoints, GPS electronically guides you from your current location directly to a desired waypoint. Once you become familiar with these units, you can set up navigation routes that lead you to a series of predetermined waypoints, or use event markers to mark schools of fish or the outlines of specific features, such as a structure or weed edge. Since GPS is satellite coordinated, it automatically programs itself, isn't affected by weather, and updates quickly.

GPS can also be a good safety device used to help guide you back to your marked access point during periods of inclement weather or darkness, or steer you clear of marked ice heaves, cracks and other areas of treacherous ice.

Full-size GPS units feature large, easy-to-view screens and separate receiving modules or antennas. Hand-held GPS units feature a built-in antenna system and are much more convenient to transport on the ice.

GATHERING INFORMATION. In addition to having maps and navigation equipment at your disposal, you can increase your chances of finding fish by keeping the following tips in mind:

• Read everything you can find concerning specific lakes in your region to help choose the most productive waters for your preferred species.

• Contact conservation wardens, fisheries biologists, researchers and technicians for current, accurate information regarding the size and condition of the specific fish population within the waters you are investigating.

• Visit local baitshop owners to see where your target species has been biting on a particular body of water and what specific techniques and baits have been most productive. In appreciation for the help, be sure to purchase a map and some basic ice tackle during your visit.

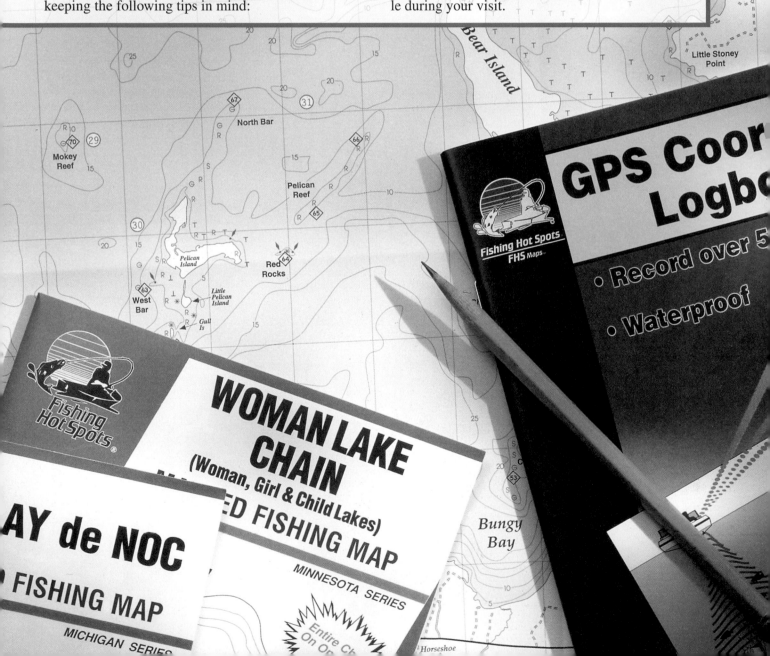

Ice-Fishing Accessories

If you look into the sled of an experienced ice fisherman, you'll notice an abundance of accessories designed to make any ice-fishing excursion more successful. While most ice anglers don't carry all the gear discussed on this page every time they head out onto the ice, at one time or another each item will be handy to have along.

SLEDS. Although many anglers simply use a large plastic child's sled to transport their gear, specialized plastic sleds with formed places to accommodate winter gear are available. Anglers traveling long distances with lots of equipment often choose deep-sided sleds with tow bars.

PAILS. Five- and six-gallon pails are an ice-fishing tradition for organizing and transporting tip-ups, rods and accessories. Some commercially produced models even feature insulated minnow buckets, storage compartments, and padded seats.

ROD HOLDERS. A variety of metal, plastic and wire rod holders are available, with the primary purpose of keeping ice rods and reels out of freezing snow and slush, while at the same time making them easily accessible.

HEATERS. Some tough winter anglers merely carry pocket hand warmers, but many opt for gas lanterns and propane heaters as outdoor sources of heat. Properly ventilated, some models may also be used in fish houses.

BAIT BUCKETS. Well insulated plastic or Styrofoam bait buckets won't freeze and keep minnows alive for a full day on the ice.

SKIMMERS. Ice chips and blowing snow can be scooped from your holes with a plastic or metal skimmer. Additions such as ice chippers or rulers stamped in the handle sections are also nice features.

GAFFS. Used to help guide large or hard-to-grasp fish onto the ice, gaffs should only be used if you plan on keeping fish.

FLOATING MINNOW NETS. To avoid dipping your hands in icy minnow buckets, use a floating minnow net or plastic scoop.

FORCEPS & CLIPPERS. Inexpensive fingernail clippers work great for cutting fishing line while forceps make it easy to remove tiny hooks from fish.

TIP-UP LIGHTS. Many winter anglers night fishing with tip-ups attach special lights, chemical light sticks, or reflector tape to the tip-up flag to see tripped flags from a distance.

DEPTHFINDERS. Clip-on depthfinder weights attach to lures or plain hooks and quickly sink to the bottom to determine depth. From here, you can accurately suspend your bobber, float, lure or bait at the desired depth above the bottom.

TIP-UP LINEMARKERS. Tip-up linemarkers are small slide or clip-on beads or bobbers that make marking your desired tip-up depth convenient. After a fish strikes and peels off line, the depth can easily be reset by locating the prerigged linemarker.

MOUTH SPREADERS. Wire mouth spreaders hold open the large, powerful mouths of toothy winter species for carefully removing hooks. Rubber-capped designs are most gentle on mouth tissues, and are best used on fish intended for release.

HOOK SHARPENERS. Down-scaled hook sharpeners are necessary to sharpen the small hooks found on ice lures.

THE EYEBUSTER™. This handy, summer-time tool for removing crusted paint from jig hook eyes is a valuable winter tool as well, especially when fumbling with cold fingers and tiny jigs.

TACKLE BOXES. From pocket-sized jig boxes with numerous small compartments to larger models designed for carrying big lures and other equipment, ice-fishing tackle boxes should feature tight-fitting covers and durable snap latches.

SPORT RADIOS. Today's hand-held radios are portable, dependable and allow anglers to communicate with one another from different parts of a lake.

GEAR BAGS. The best bags feature water resistant fabric, outside and inside storage pockets, and a wide opening to easily see and access equipment.

Winter Gamefish Techniques

Sunfish

When it comes to ice fishing and universal popularity, the sunfish wins hands down.

Why? Geographically, they're found throughout much of the North American ice-fishing climate, flourish in numerous aquatic environments throughout the winter, put up a strong tussle on light ice tackle and, because they feed actively beneath the ice, usually aren't difficult to catch.

Bluegill

Collectively the sunfish family includes several species, but when it comes to ice fishing, the two primary targets are bluegills and pumpkinseeds. Bluegills (above) have light blue lower gill covers and a distinctive dark blue lobe on the upper gill; pumpkinseeds (opposite page) have a colorful lattice of blue-green and red-orange flecks lining their flanks, and an iridescent, crimson-lined dark blue upper gill cover.

While both species feed actively beneath the ice, their small, circular mouths limit the size of their prey. Fortunately this physical limitation is offset by their sensitive lateral line that senses even the slightest wrinkle of movement in their prey. In addition, the sunfish's keen eyesight can identify even the tiniest aquatic organisms, and swift maneuvering capability allows them to deftly attack microscopic plankton, tiny aquatic insects, invertebrates and small minnows.

HABITAT AND FEEDING PATTERNS

Sunfish adapt to and flourish in many winter environments. You'll find them beneath the ice of small farm ponds, shallow sand and gravel pits, natural and man-made lakes and an intricate maze of frozen river backwaters.

Weedy shallows and mid-depth weed edges are common winter habitat. Green, broad-leaved vegetation such as curly leaf cabbage or thick stands of reeds provide substrate for a variety of food items, shaded protection from predators, ambush points from which to attack prey, plus furnish oxygen. The presence of slight current from an incoming stream or spring helps circulate water beneath the ice and is also a bonus. Expect sunfish in clear water to relate closely to the densest, shadiest stands of vegetation. In stained or dark water, they'll hold more loosely along its edges.

Like many other species, small sunfish often group in shallow, more dense stands of weeds. Given an abundance of food, larger sunfish may temporarily hold in such areas, but are more likely to school around deep weed edges. If ice and snow cover are thick enough or water clarity marred enough to restrict sunlight from reaching these weeds, they turn brown, deteriorate and decay. The resulting loss of cover, food and oxygen sends sunfish into deeper water, or causes them to suspend over deep open-water regions.

While sunfish feed all winter, many ice anglers prefer to fish sunfish just after the ice thickens enough to walk on, a period commonly referred to as first ice; and again just before the ice melts, a time called last ice—periods when sunfish are most likely schooled and feeding in shallow, weedy bays or backwaters.

Most feeding activity occurs during the day, with the first light of morning and last light of the afternoon often producing best.

Pumpkinseed ready to be unhooked

57

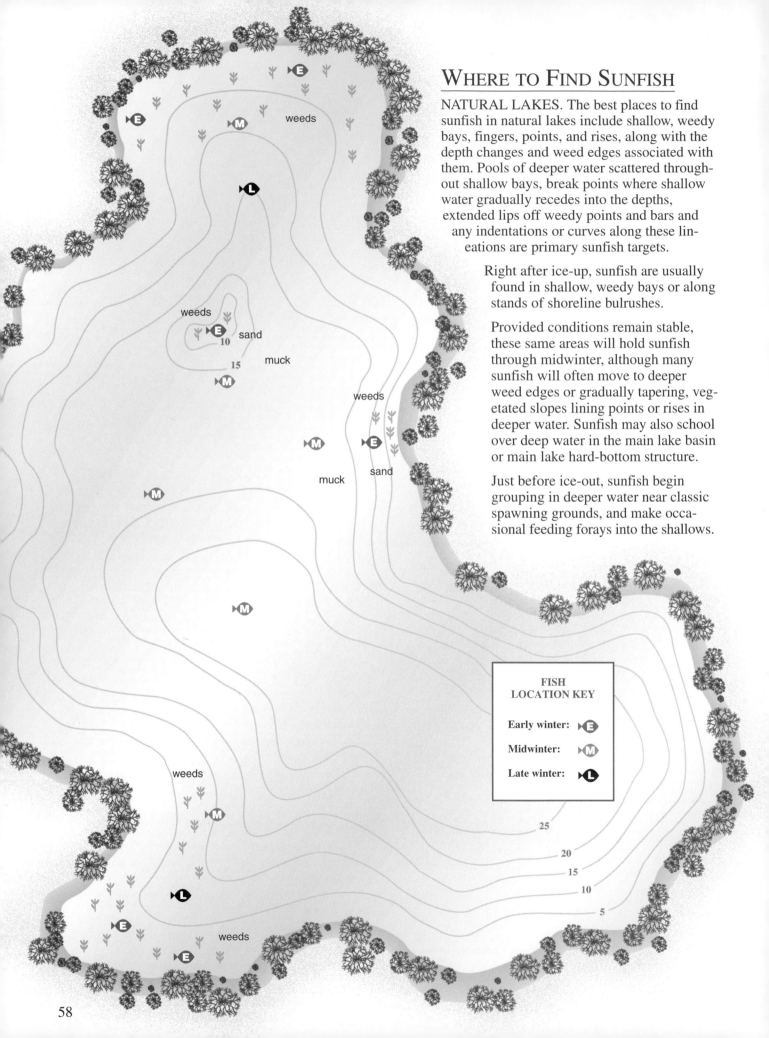

WHERE TO FIND SUNFISH

NATURAL LAKES. The best places to find sunfish in natural lakes include shallow, weedy bays, fingers, points, and rises, along with the depth changes and weed edges associated with them. Pools of deeper water scattered throughout shallow bays, break points where shallow water gradually recedes into the depths, extended lips off weedy points and bars and any indentations or curves along these lineations are primary sunfish targets.

Right after ice-up, sunfish are usually found in shallow, weedy bays or along stands of shoreline bulrushes.

Provided conditions remain stable, these same areas will hold sunfish through midwinter, although many sunfish will often move to deeper weed edges or gradually tapering, vegetated slopes lining points or rises in deeper water. Sunfish may also school over deep water in the main lake basin or main lake hard-bottom structure.

Just before ice-out, sunfish begin grouping in deeper water near classic spawning grounds, and make occasional feeding forays into the shallows.

FISH LOCATION KEY

Early winter: E

Midwinter: M

Late winter: L

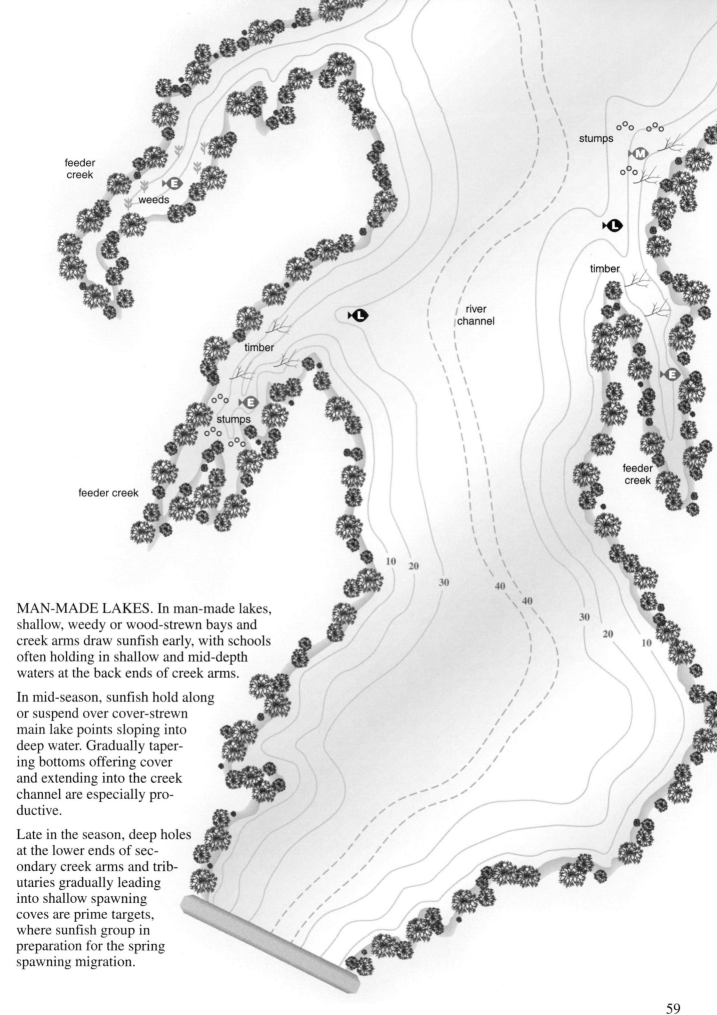

feeder
creek

weeds

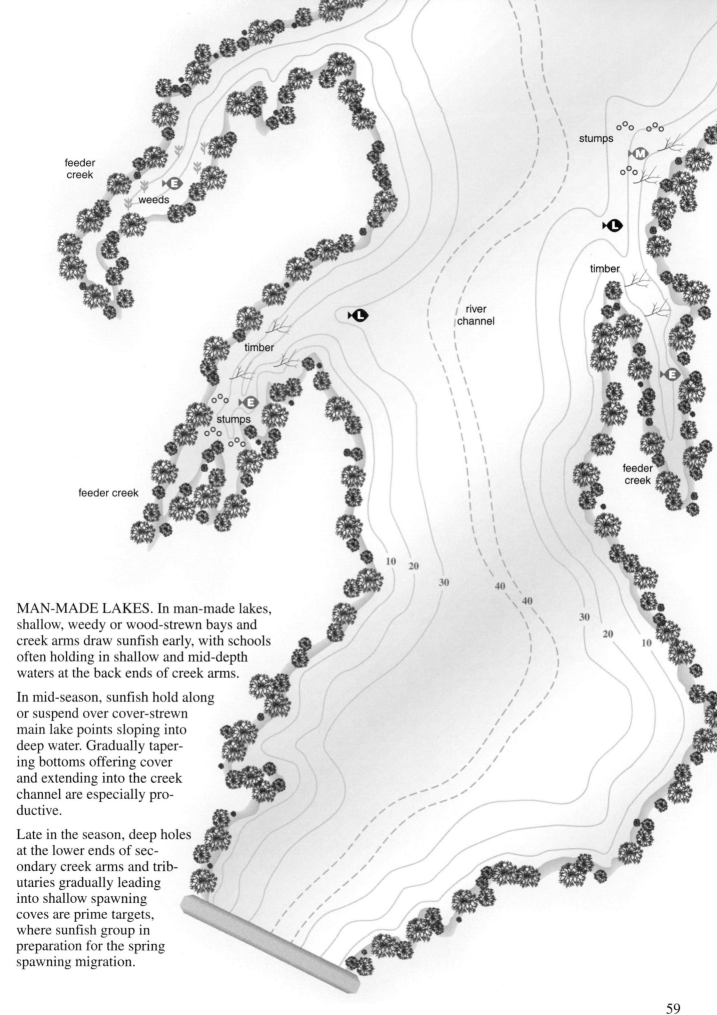E

stumps

M

L

timber

L

river
channel

timber

stumps

E

feeder creek

E

feeder
creek

10 20

30

40

40

30

20

10

MAN-MADE LAKES. In man-made lakes, shallow, weedy or wood-strewn bays and creek arms draw sunfish early, with schools often holding in shallow and mid-depth waters at the back ends of creek arms.

In mid-season, sunfish hold along or suspend over cover-strewn main lake points sloping into deep water. Gradually tapering bottoms offering cover and extending into the creek channel are especially productive.

Late in the season, deep holes at the lower ends of secondary creek arms and tributaries gradually leading into shallow spawning coves are prime targets, where sunfish group in preparation for the spring spawning migration.

PONDS AND PITS. While often small, don't underestimate the potential of ponds, especially at first ice, when panfish feed eagerly. Deeper holes within weedy shallows, weedy fingers, points and rises offering definitive depth changes and weed edges will virtually always hold active sunnies. In pits, vegetation is again the key to finding first ice sunfish when available, but weeds are often lacking or absent. If so, look for steep walls with overhanging rocks or shallow sections of broken rock to attract sunfish.

In mid-season, many shallow, weedy ponds become light starved, and as weeds die and decompose, using oxygen, sunfish suspend over deep water. Areas of flowing water, such as near an inlet, outlet or spring may also be good. Pits typically sustain better oxygen concentration, and although sunfish often continue to use the same overhanging and shallow rock outcroppings for cover, they may suspend.

Late in the season, pond sunfish return to a more active feeding state. Look for them around newly developing shallow weeds lining the pond. In pits, sunfish often suspend or hold near shallow shoreline rock.

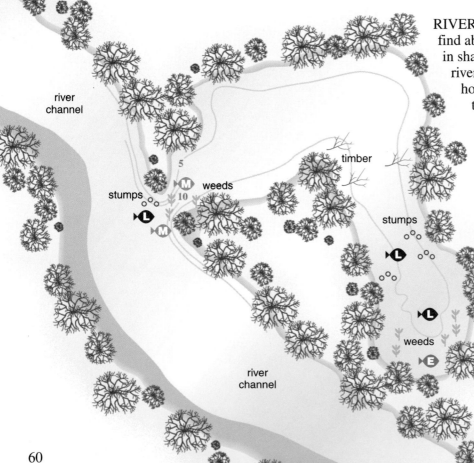

RIVER BACKWATERS. Early season will find abundant conglomerations of sunfish in shallow, weedy or stumpy, log-jammed river backwaters. The edges of deeper holes in such cover are primary targets to seek, just be sure the backwaters aren't secluded from the main channel where they may be cut off from current flow or isolated from the river completely in the event water levels drop.

During mid-season, search for deep eddies at the mouth of mid-depth backwaters graced with a hint of current. Those featuring weed growth or tangles of flooded brush are generally most productive.

By late ice, these deep eddies continue to hold sunfish, but given the right conditions, periodic movements back into the mid-depth backwater cover may occur.

How To Catch Sunfish

Due to the sunfish's small mouth and winter hankering for small food items, winter fishing tackle begins with small lures and baits that best represent their natural forage.

Traditionally, ice anglers caught sunfish by suspending #10 and smaller hooks, jigs or ice flies with 4-pound test monofilament line below tiny, fixed bobbers (right). Small split shot was usually used to neutrally balance the bobbers so even the slightest sunfish bites could be seen. Some veteran sunfish anglers preferred tiny, spoon-shaped teardrop lures with fins or rubber legs to create flash, sound and a wiggling action. Hackled wet flies, because of their slow drop rate when jigged, were also used extensively. Once a sunfish was hooked, an angler pulled it in by hand.

While most modern ice anglers opt for high-tech rods and reels, lighter lines and no bobbers, the lures that were popular in the past still catch fish today.

Perhaps more important than the exact style of lure you chose is the addition of fresh live bait to the

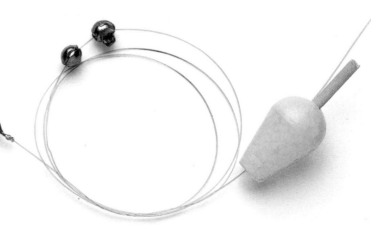

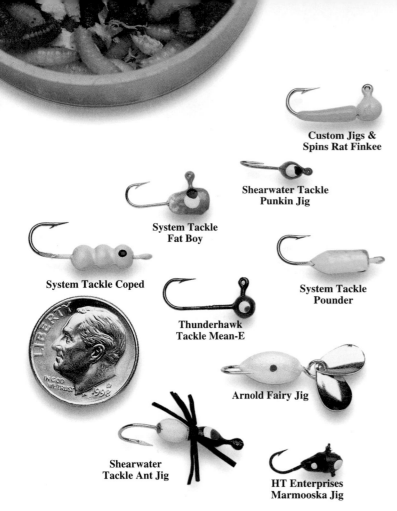

Custom Jigs & Spins Rat Finkee

Shearwater Tackle Punkin Jig

System Tackle Fat Boy

System Tackle Coped

Thunderhawk Tackle Mean-E

System Tackle Pounder

Arnold Fairy Jig

Shearwater Tackle Ant Jig

HT Enterprises Marmooska Jig

Waxworm

Eurolarvae

overall presentation. The scent trail provided by juicy grubs and maggots such as waxworms, spikes, mousies, poppers or Eurolarvae help instigate more strikes, and cause fish to hold on longer, resulting in better hooking.

When using waxworms, be sure to thread it straight on your hook, much as you would thread a plastic twister-tail grub on a jig head (above). This rigging allows the lure and worm to fall naturally without twisting your line.

Eurolarvae-style grubs are a bit more difficult to rig correctly. Start by gently rolling the grub between your finger tips. This causes the grub to shorten its body and get fatter. Then, identify the blunt end of the grub and the little tuft of skin raised on one edge of this blunt end. Gently impale the hook tip through this tuft of skin leaving the lively bait squirm (above). If you've hooked it correctly, no body fluids from the grub will appear. Don't be concerned about the hook showing, the main goal is to keep the bait alive and wiggling naturally. Many ice-fishing experts flatten the barbs on their panfish lures to make rigging Eurolarvae easier.

Sight-Fishing Secrets

Experienced ice anglers use the term "sight fishing" to describe the method used when sunfish can be visually located through an ice hole then fooled into hitting a lure. The practice is best accomplished by sitting in a darkened fish house on a bright day. In a clear water environment, sunfish can easily be seen below, and watching their reaction to your presentation can become quite educational, even fixating.

For best results, search for an open pocket in green, mid-depth vegetation, or create an opening by pushing your ice auger into the weeds and removing a patch of vegetation. After the sediments have settled, sunfish will move in to feed on the disturbed food items.

Select a small, slow-falling lure you can easily work with a slight, finesse quivering-style motion, and spool with light, fresh line to allow maximum lure control and eliminate spinning. Most anglers prefer short sight-fishing rods such as the 16-inch Thorne Bros. Sweet Pea (p. 31). To minimize lower back strain, extend your arm out and turn the rod tip toward your body to keep the lure working directly below. From here, you can adjust the size, color and movement of your lure to the fish's demonstrated preference.

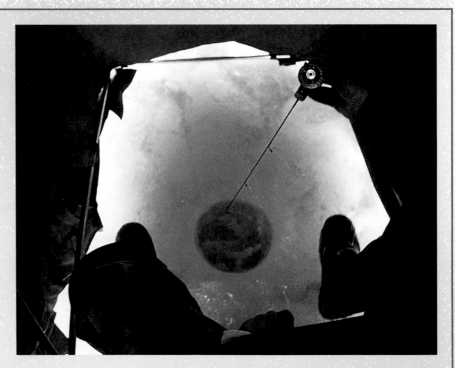

In addition to live bait, it is extremely important to use a thin, straight, limp monofilament line with no kinks or curls that reduce your ability to control the lure's subtle movements. This is especially true if you fish tiny ice flies without a float or micro shot.

Special ice rods have been designed in the past few years specifically for catching sunfish. The best models feature a light, sensitive tip to detect strikes yet enough backbone to set the hook into a big sunfish, even when fishing in depths over 15 feet. Tiny spinning reels with quality drag systems are paired with these rods to make deadly ice-fishing combinations.

Many veteran ice fishermen, regardless of the sunfish's activity levels, prefer to drill small, 4-inch holes, which are easier to cut, promoting mobility, and more difficult for sunfish to turn within to escape. Small holes also reduce the chance of fish seeing you in shallow or clear water; some savvy anglers even kick ice skimmings in the water to avoid being spotted by fish and limit the amount of sunlight going down the hole.

PRODUCTIVE JIGGING METHODS. Early and late in the day, or during times when sunfish are feeding intently, they can easily be teased into striking a broad up and down, up and down, pause, sequence with traditional, vertical-style ice jigs.

During midday or periods when sunfish aren't feeding as strongly, you'll have to work at agitating them into striking. Now, more subtle, gradual, lift-fall quivering motion with horizontal jigs becomes important. Be sure your line is straight, your bait is fresh and tipped in a straight, horizontal position to prevent spinning. Such finesse techniques are especially productive in shallow or clear water.

In deep or dark water, or during periods of inactivity, go with heavier jigs for better lure control, and fish with a more aggressive, "pounding" technique (right), popularized by ice pro Dave Genz. The goal is to attract their attention, then trigger an angry response you might not otherwise get with a gentle, finesse approach. When fishing this way, Dave prefers lures of horizontal design such as the System Tackle Fat Boy, or specialized, flat-topped designs like System Tackle Pounders. These lures are "flasher friendly," meaning they show up well on your sonar.

Obviously with any of these rigs or movements, knowing how to use your sonar is a tremendous help, as you can identify schools of sunfish holding in or along the edges of cover, even sunfish suspended in deep, open water, then witness their reaction to your fishing lures and movements. From here, you can make style and cadence changes as necessary to increase your catch.

A 2-pound-plus sunfish taken by "pounding" an ice jig

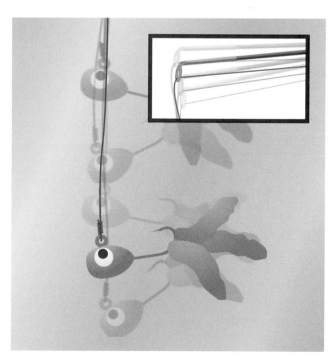

THE POUNDING TECHNIQUE is best accomplished with a stiff graphite panfish rod, thin-diameter monofilament and a relatively heavy ice jig. The goal is to rapidly "pound" the rod tip (inset) in such a way as to make the jig quiver up and down without spinning. In deep water, where line stretch is maximized, the rod must be pounded aggressively to make the jig quiver appropriately.

Crappies

White Crappie

Of all species caught through the ice, crappies are undoubtedly one of the most popular.

Like other members of the sunfish family, crappies inhabit frozen waters throughout most of the heavily ice-fished regions of North America, with the exception of the deeper, colder waters of higher mountain elevations and northern Canada. Crappies also have the capability to grow to 2 pounds or more, are relatively easy to catch, and put up a scrappy fight.

The black crappie (opposite page) is most commonly taken by ice anglers and identified by a varied, dark blotched pattern along their sides. White crappies (above) can be differentiated from black crappies by vertical columns of dark speckles arranged in regular columns along their flanks.

Both species feed all winter long, and demonstrate varied diets. Featuring a fine mesh of closely spaced gill rakers allowing them to efficiently graze on plankton and, with relatively large mouths, crappies can easily feed on aquatic insect larvae, crustaceans and small baitfish.

HABITAT AND FEEDING PATTERNS

Although crappies are considered easy to catch, many ice anglers also concede they're not always so easy to find. Waters featuring an overabundant population of small crappies may not be challenging, but ice anglers looking for quality fish will find crappies worthy foe.

An incessant wandering breed, crappies may densely school in deep, open water siphoning plankton one winter day, then scattered along a shallow weedline chasing baitfish or a deep rock reef feeding on crustaceans the next.

Since winter habitat and forage may be comprised of such a wide range of variables, ice anglers must be prepared to move often while searching for crappies. Try assembling a listing of waters with solid crappie populations, then note hard-bottom areas offering plenty of weedy or woody baitfish-attracting cover such as thick bulrush stands or sunken timber—the crappies preferred shallow-water habitat—preferably near deep, open water regions where they may suspend to hoard plankton, or deep, hard-bottom regions that may hold baitfish or crustaceans. Then be prepared to fish them all.

Provided food and oxygen are adequate, small, stunted crappies often remain in shallow weeds throughout the winter, while sizable crappies are more likely to be found holding along deeper weed edges, cover and structures or suspended over deep water.

Crappies feed throughout the winter, but few ice anglers will argue the benefit of fishing crappies early and late in the season when forage is most concentrated in shallow cover, and so are the crappies.

The most intense winter feeding periods occur during periods of twilight and darkness, with the hours just prior to and after sunrise and sunset generally being most productive.

Angler adding another black crappie to his catch

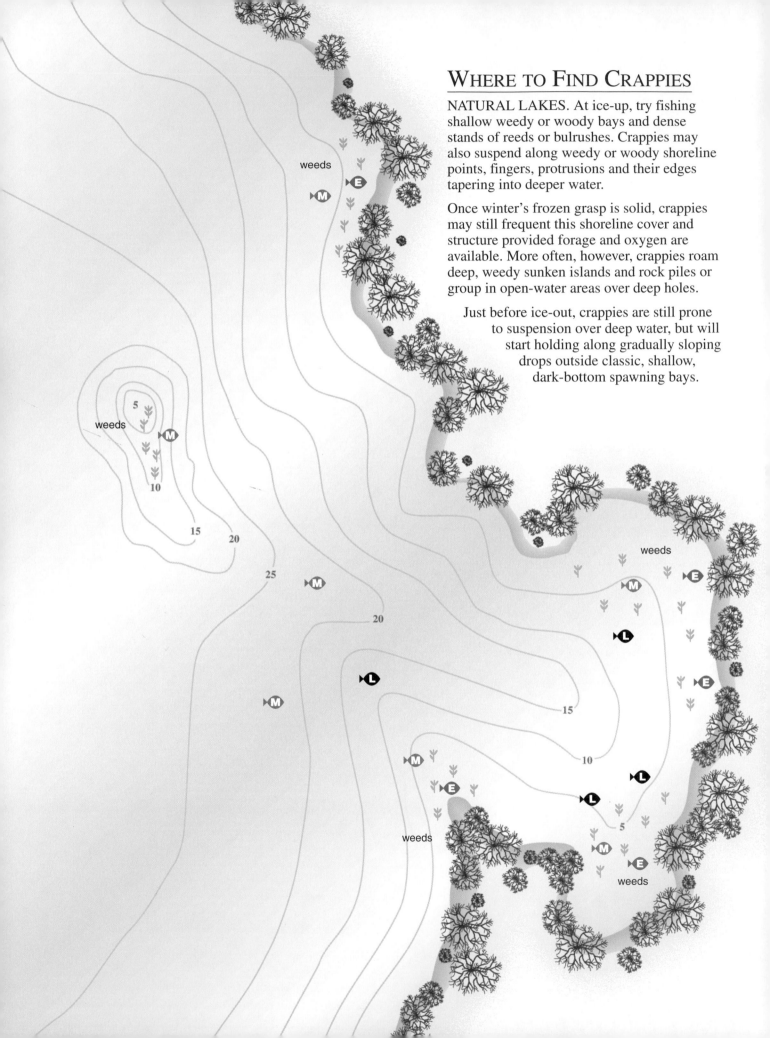

WHERE TO FIND CRAPPIES

NATURAL LAKES. At ice-up, try fishing shallow weedy or woody bays and dense stands of reeds or bulrushes. Crappies may also suspend along weedy or woody shoreline points, fingers, protrusions and their edges tapering into deeper water.

Once winter's frozen grasp is solid, crappies may still frequent this shoreline cover and structure provided forage and oxygen are available. More often, however, crappies roam deep, weedy sunken islands and rock piles or group in open-water areas over deep holes.

Just before ice-out, crappies are still prone to suspension over deep water, but will start holding along gradually sloping drops outside classic, shallow, dark-bottom spawning bays.

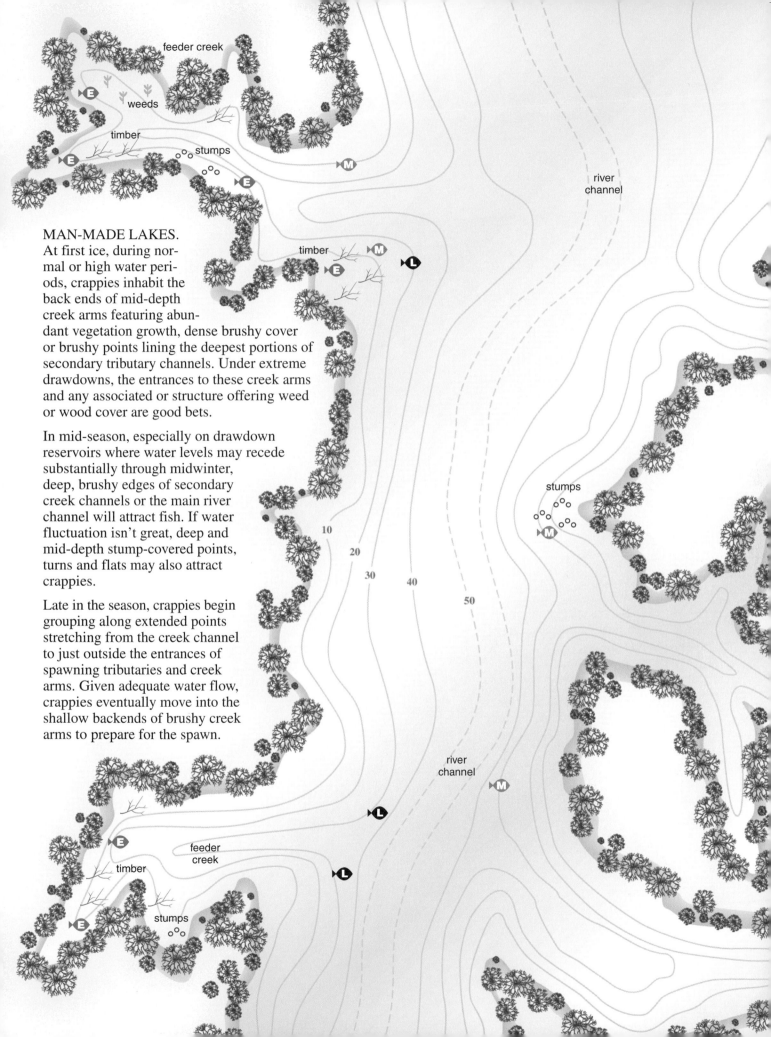

feeder creek

E

weeds

timber

stumps

M

E

MAN-MADE LAKES.
At first ice, during nor-
mal or high water peri-
ods, crappies inhabit the
back ends of mid-depth
creek arms featuring abun-
dant vegetation growth, dense brushy cover
or brushy points lining the deepest portions of
secondary tributary channels. Under extreme
drawdowns, the entrances to these creek arms
and any associated or structure offering weed
or wood cover are good bets.

In mid-season, especially on drawdown
reservoirs where water levels may recede
substantially through midwinter,
deep, brushy edges of secondary
creek channels or the main river
channel will attract fish. If water
fluctuation isn't great, deep and
mid-depth stump-covered points,
turns and flats may also attract
crappies.

Late in the season, crappies begin
grouping along extended points
stretching from the creek channel
to just outside the entrances of
spawning tributaries and creek
arms. Given adequate water flow,
crappies eventually move into the
shallow backends of brushy creek
arms to prepare for the spawn.

timber

M

E

L

river
channel

stumps

M

10

20

30

40

50

river
channel

M

L

E

feeder
creek

timber

L

E

stumps

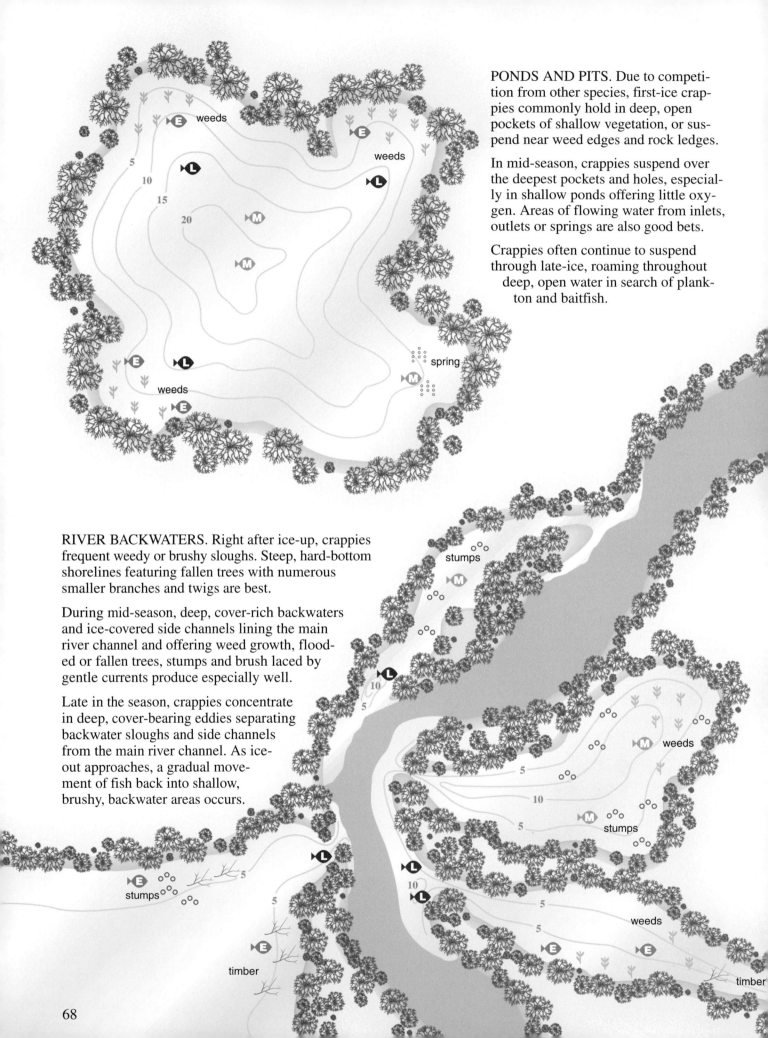

PONDS AND PITS. Due to competition from other species, first-ice crappies commonly hold in deep, open pockets of shallow vegetation, or suspend near weed edges and rock ledges.

In mid-season, crappies suspend over the deepest pockets and holes, especially in shallow ponds offering little oxygen. Areas of flowing water from inlets, outlets or springs are also good bets.

Crappies often continue to suspend through late-ice, roaming throughout deep, open water in search of plankton and baitfish.

RIVER BACKWATERS. Right after ice-up, crappies frequent weedy or brushy sloughs. Steep, hard-bottom shorelines featuring fallen trees with numerous smaller branches and twigs are best.

During mid-season, deep, cover-rich backwaters and ice-covered side channels lining the main river channel and offering weed growth, flooded or fallen trees, stumps and brush laced by gentle currents produce especially well.

Late in the season, crappies concentrate in deep, cover-bearing eddies separating backwater sloughs and side channels from the main river channel. As ice-out approaches, a gradual movement of fish back into shallow, brushy, backwater areas occurs.

weeds

weeds

weeds

spring

stumps

stumps

weeds

stumps

stumps

timber

weeds

timber

HOW TO CATCH CRAPPIES

Basic winter crappie tackle consists of a splitshot, small shiner or fathead minnow suspended beneath a small bobber pegged on 2- to 4-pound monofilament leading to a light-action ice rod. In shallow, clear water, watch your minnow and set the bait just above any weed or wood cover for a delicate, shallow-water presentation. In deeper water, use slip-bobber designs, sonar and additional shot as required to achieve the same presentation accuracy.

Ice anglers fishing through difficult daytime periods must be willing to move in search of active fish. For ease of mobility, these anglers often forego toting heavy, sloshing minnow buckets in favor of a small tin of grubs, and substitute small balsa slip-floats in their bobber rigs.

Either way, most modern ice experts emphasize the importance of neutrally balancing today's floats with enough carefully placed micro-shot so light-biting crappies feel minimal unnatural resistance when striking.

With trends in ice fishing leading anglers more toward the unexplored depths of deep-water structure and the growing popularity of spinning tackle for hard-water fishing, standard "peg" bobbers and floats of yesteryear are increasingly giving way to use of slip-bobbers.

Slip-bobbers consist of standard bobber and float designs, but feature a narrow passage through the center to accommodate your line. Instead of pegging the line securely at the desired depth setting, line is allowed to slip through the float as the lure or bait sinks, until a small stop set at a predetermined depth on the line catches at the top of the passage. This technique allows precision depth control and, since the small stop can also be reeled through the guides of an ice rod, slip-bobbers are popular with winter crappie anglers fishing deep water.

While a simple minnow and bobber system is most effective early in the season when residual numbers of baitfish may still form a reliable food source, the situation soon changes. As winter sets in, baitfish availability wanes and crappies begin turning more to plankton as a primary food supply. As this transpires, a gradual progression toward smaller, grub-tipped teardrops and horizontal jigs occurs. For maximum attraction and better jigging control, many

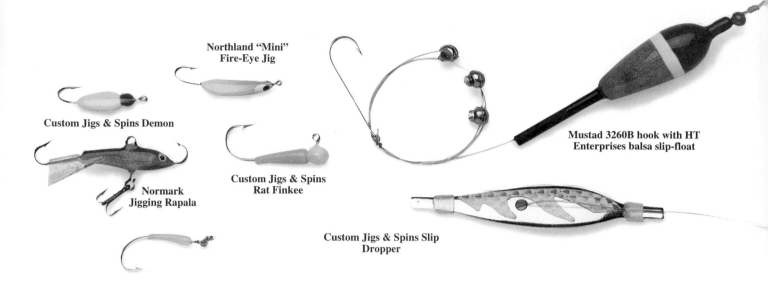

Custom Jigs & Spins Demon

Northland "Mini" Fire-Eye Jig

Normark Jigging Rapala

Custom Jigs & Spins Rat Finkee

Custom Jigs & Spins Slip Dropper

Mustad 3260B hook with HT Enterprises balsa slip-float

experts discontinue use of bobbers, and choose instead to jig "tight line" with light-action rods, small jigs and fresh, lively maggots.

In deep water, use heavier, phosphorescent jigs to provide improved lure control and better visibility to fish. When fishing shallow water, lighter, slower falling, more delicate natural-looking lures are desired. Larger shiny, minnow-imitating, swimming-style lures like jigging minnows, spoons and minnow-tipped jigs can also be productive during periods when crappies are feeding on minnows, and may also be a good way to draw attention and trigger strikes during challenging daytime hours.

However, ice fishing pro Dave Genz has noted minnows and minnow-imitating baits are most productive at sunrise and sundown, when crappies are adjusting their eyes to transient light conditions.

Dave also maintains that grub-tipped jigs, properly worked to tease daytime crappies into striking, will outfish minnows 3:1 and are more effective when trying to entice finicky daytime crappies.

A good way to increase your catch when jig fishing for finicky crappies is to use a dropper hook. First, tie a 6-inch piece of 2- to 4-pound test monofilament to the bend of a jig's hook. Second, attach a #10 to #14 maggot-tipped hook to the dropper line. Crappies that don't want the larger offering of the ice jig often suck in the tiny hook with the single maggot.

With any of these methods, ice anglers must remember crappies feature micro-thin membrane around their mouths. The best practice for successful hooking is to keep your hooks sharp, and set the hook with no more than a mere, firm flip of your wrist. Set too hard, and hooks may tear loose.

Tips for Catching Crappies

HOOK minnows just behind the dorsal fin (above) or through the tail when fished below a bobber and through the lips or eye sockets when jigged.

KEEP a good bend in the rod while fighting crappies, or for that matter, any species of fish. If you give crappies slack line, the hook may slip out.

PRODUCTIVE JIGGING METHODS. With any precision winter crappie jigging presentation, the use of sonar is important to identify the depth crappies are holding, and depth they're most likely to strike. Don't be fooled into believing the most productive jigging depth is right where the fish are holding. Crappies are often prone to striking lures placed above them. Use your sonar to establish a pattern each time you fish.

Also note that crappies holding above or below the school are typically the largest fish. They may be harder to catch, but the rewards of targeting them are worth the extra effort. The following paragraphs describe how to get the most out of jigging with a variety of lure and bait combinations.

BOBBER RIG. Dabbling a minnow beneath a float is most productive during periods of changing light. Movement can be reserved to the natural struggling action of the minnow, but occasional lift-drops to promote minnow movement and periodic depth setting changes are recommended.

MINNOW-TIPPED JIG. A simple, progressive rising or dropping motion from just below the fish to just above or vice-versa is often all that's required to instigate strikes. Bites can be light as a simple tightening or slackening line, or obvious as a distinct, rod-bending take. Note if the most strikes are occurring during the rise or fall, and fish accordingly.

GRUB-TIPPED JIG. When fishing grub-tipped jigs during the day, you'll want to work your bait in an attempt to trick or anger crappies into striking. Productive jigging rhythms might vary from a gentle, sunfish-style, light quivering motion to a more aggressive "pounding" action. Either way, rigging your grub horizontally is critical or line twist is eminent, especially when fishing deep.

SWIMMING LURE. To take advantage of the movement these lures offer, regular, sharp lifts followed by sudden drops of your rod tip will be necessary. The resulting slack line allows the lure to glide to the side before returning to its original position. Vary the number and height of these lift-drop motions to determine what brings the best results.

SPOON. A slow-dropping, flat-bodied spoon tipped with a hint of bait makes a terrific daytime crappie presentation. The combination of tempting flash plus natural smell and taste triggers strikes even during the most challenging fishing conditions. The slow drop also makes determining the best strike depth more obvious.

Lights, Camera, Action!

Since winter crappies are most likely to feed during low-light periods, the use of phosphorescent glow jigs and bodies often helps crappies close in on a bait. Many of today's nighttime crappie experts employ a standard camera flash to intensify this brightness and make it last longer. By wrapping tin foil around the camera flash, the phosphorescent paint is subjected to a sudden, very direct, intense flash of brilliant white light, which results in a powerful, long-lasting glow.

Walleyes & Saugers

Sauger

Walleyes and saugers have recently bathed in the limelight of a swelling fishing scene. Once the topic of a few magazine articles, some periodicals are now dedicated solely to walleyes and saugers. Walleye fishing tournaments have become popularized by large purse winnings. Manufacturers have responded with tackle specifically aimed at improving anglers' walleye catches. And with this remarkable transformation, there has been a tremendous resurgence of interest in ice fishing for walleyes and saugers.

Some anglers might suggest this is because strong populations of walleyes and saugers exist in waters encompassing virtually all of the North American ice-fishing scene. Many argue it's the thrill of watching tip-up flags trip, or the feel of smashing strikes on an ice rod. But no one will deny the draw of a sweet, fresh walleye or sauger fillet taken from winter's icy waters, carefully seasoned in a tasty coating and fried to a steaming, mouth-watering golden-brown crisp.

Walleyes (opposite page) can easily be identified by their pale, golden-green sides, whitish-gold bellies, a black spot at the rear of the dorsal fin, and a distinct white tip on their lower tail. Saugers (above) are distinguished by their brownish-grey sides, often blotted with darker brown patches spread across their flanks, and a pattern of distinct black spots on their dorsal fin.

Walleyes and saugers are cool-water, schooling fish that remain quite active beneath winter's icy covering. Their characteristic, light-sensitive eyes enable them to see well even during low-light or dark conditions, and productive evening "bites" are common.

HABITAT AND FEEDING PATTERNS

Although walleyes and saugers are historically creatures of a river environment, thanks to widespread stocking, solid populations have been sustained in many natural and man-made lakes.

Walleyes and saugers have often been coined by much of the ice-angling fraternity as inhabitants of deep, hard-bottom structure, largely because of their affinity for deep rocky flats, humps, bars and points. Ice experts have also noted bulrush beds on shallow and mid-depth structures are productive during early

season, and mid-depth, gradually sloping drops are prominent staging areas for schools awaiting up-river spring spawning migrations.

In fact, provided food is available, oxygen concentrations aren't limiting and sunlight penetration isn't direct, shallow stumpfields, gravel or rock flats, weedy shallows and mid-depth weed edges are typical winter walleye habitat, especially early or late in the season. Since walleyes and sauger have such light-sensitive eyes, shallow-water fish usually hold tight to cover or move into deeper water during the day, then stalk shallow prey by moonlight.

During bright daytime periods, especially in deep, clear lakes, walleyes relate to more stereotypical, deep-water patterns. Rocky, main basin points, humps and shoals and their edges are good places to try. Still, these schools may be very mobile. Not only are they likely to drop deeper during bright parts of the day and rise at night, but they may also migrate from structure to structure, searching for food.

Walleyes and saugers remain active throughout the winter, but most action occurs right after ice-up and just prior to ice-out.

First ice typically provides the best fishing, especially for big fish, as larger females are gorging themselves to enhance egg production. By mid-season, action slows. Ice anglers hold a variety of opinions to substantiate this behavior, but most attribute slow midwinter action to increasingly cold water temperatures, reduced baitfish populations, and lowered oxygen concentrations. Egg production is also no longer a primary concern. By late season, action typically rebounds as forage availability, water temperatures and oxygen concentrations increase.

Since walleyes and saugers have light-sensitive eyes and a feeding advantage over other predators and prey during periods of darkness, the most intense winter feeding forays take place during low-light and evening periods. Most winter trophies are taken during wee hours of the morning, with many experts believing full moon periods provide the best opportunity for quality fish.

Fisherman gaffing a walleye destined for the dinner table

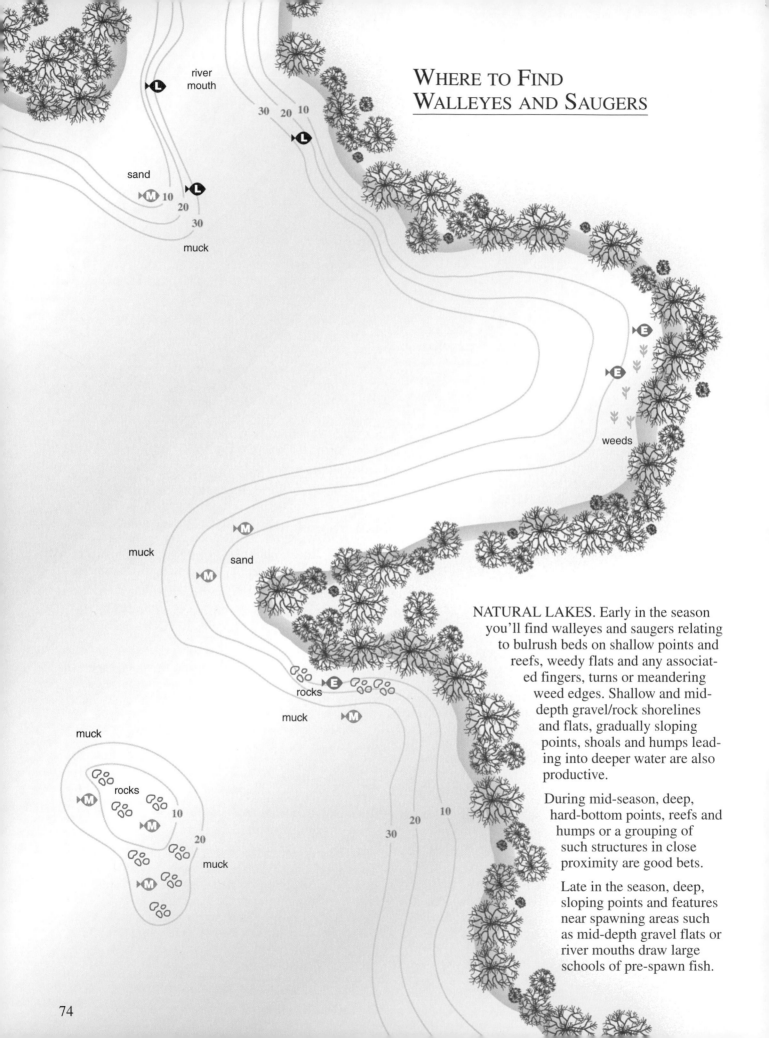

river
mouth

30 20 10

sand
10
20
30
muck

muck

sand

weeds

muck

rocks

muck

muck

rocks

10

20

muck

WHERE TO FIND WALLEYES AND SAUGERS

NATURAL LAKES. Early in the season you'll find walleyes and saugers relating to bulrush beds on shallow points and reefs, weedy flats and any associated fingers, turns or meandering weed edges. Shallow and mid-depth gravel/rock shorelines and flats, gradually sloping points, shoals and humps leading into deeper water are also productive.

During mid-season, deep, hard-bottom points, reefs and humps or a grouping of such structures in close proximity are good bets.

Late in the season, deep, sloping points and features near spawning areas such as mid-depth gravel flats or river mouths draw large schools of pre-spawn fish.

20 10

30

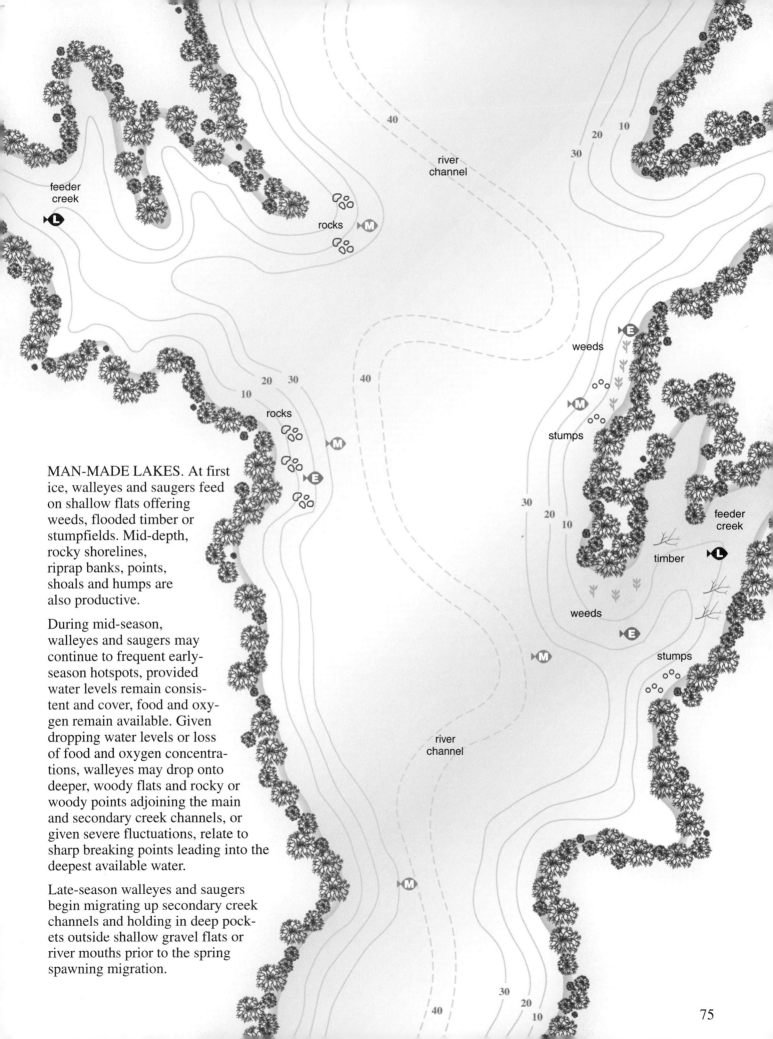

40

river
channel

20 **10**

30

feeder
creek

►L

rocks ►M

20 **30**

40

10

weeds ►E

rocks

►M

MAN-MADE LAKES. At first
ice, walleyes and saugers feed
on shallow flats offering
weeds, flooded timber or
stumpfields. Mid-depth,
rocky shorelines,
riprap banks, points,
shoals and humps are
also productive.

►M

stumps

feeder
creek

timber ►L

During mid-season,
walleyes and saugers may
continue to frequent early-
season hotspots, provided
water levels remain consistent and cover, food and oxygen remain available. Given
dropping water levels or loss
of food and oxygen concentrations, walleyes may drop onto
deeper, woody flats and rocky or
woody points adjoining the main
and secondary creek channels, or
given severe fluctuations, relate to
sharp breaking points leading into the
deepest available water.

►E

30

20

10

weeds

►E

stumps

►M

river
channel

Late-season walleyes and saugers
begin migrating up secondary creek
channels and holding in deep pockets outside shallow gravel flats or
river mouths prior to the spring
spawning migration.

►M

30 **20**

40 **10**

75

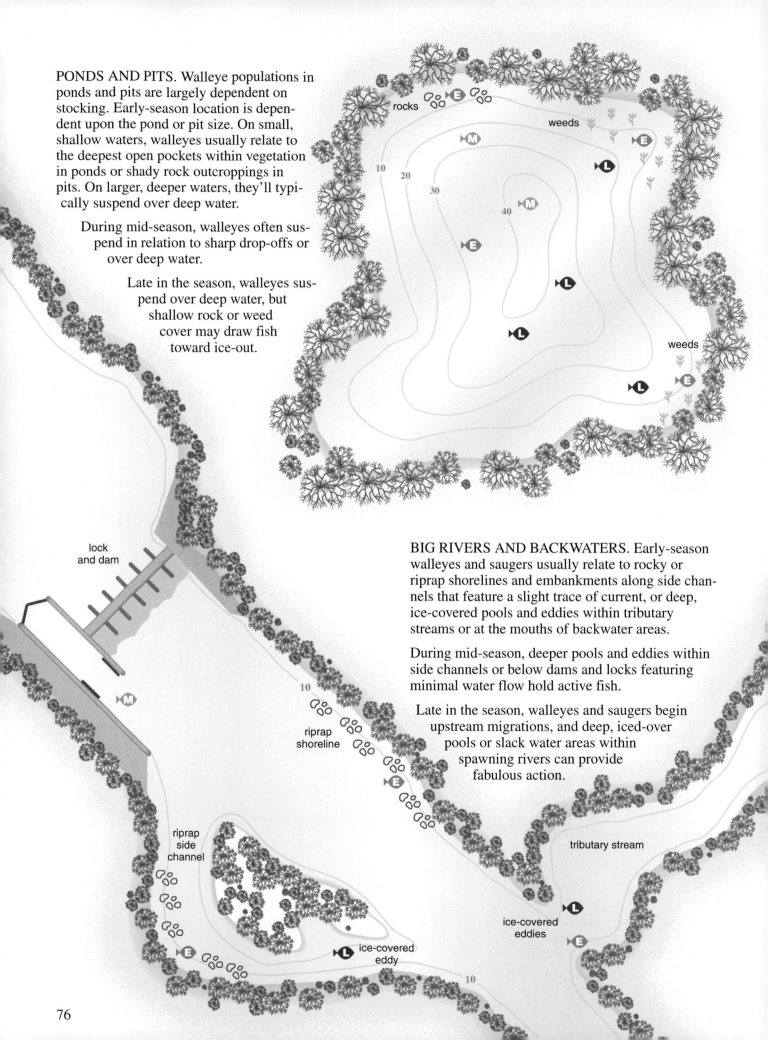

PONDS AND PITS. Walleye populations in ponds and pits are largely dependent on stocking. Early-season location is dependent upon the pond or pit size. On small, shallow waters, walleyes usually relate to the deepest open pockets within vegetation in ponds or shady rock outcroppings in pits. On larger, deeper waters, they'll typically suspend over deep water.

During mid-season, walleyes often suspend in relation to sharp drop-offs or over deep water.

Late in the season, walleyes suspend over deep water, but shallow rock or weed cover may draw fish toward ice-out.

rocks

weeds

10
20
30
40

weeds

lock and dam

BIG RIVERS AND BACKWATERS. Early-season walleyes and saugers usually relate to rocky or riprap shorelines and embankments along side channels that feature a slight trace of current, or deep, ice-covered pools and eddies within tributary streams or at the mouths of backwater areas.

During mid-season, deeper pools and eddies within side channels or below dams and locks featuring minimal water flow hold active fish.

Late in the season, walleyes and saugers begin upstream migrations, and deep, iced-over pools or slack water areas within spawning rivers can provide fabulous action.

10

riprap shoreline

riprap side channel

tributary stream

ice-covered eddies

ice-covered eddy

10

HOW TO CATCH WALLEYES AND SAUGER

Winter walleye and sauger presentation can be tricky, as both species are known for their odd, light-biting feeding habits.

TIP-UPS. Experienced ice anglers usually use 15- to 20-pound braided dacron for backing, then attach monofilament or thin, wire leaders graced with just enough split shot to lower a hooked minnow to the desired depth.

The most popular walleye tip-up rig involves a strong, thin-diameter wire or monofilament leader, split shot and minnow-tipped hook. Experts have also learned that adding small, metal or plastic spinners to the leader and painting the hook with bright or glow colors adds fish-attracting color and flash. Colorful beads, bits of yarn, pork rind and plastic trailers offer similar benefits.

The popularity of wind-activated tip-ups and tip-downs has grown tremendously in recent years. Since such tip-ups are capable of jigging your bait, standard minnow rigs are effective because the additional movement draws attention and inspires strikes.

Since wind tip-ups such as the HT Windlass can be adjusted to move with varying motion, the use of grub-tipped jigs and minnow-rigged spoons has also caught on. Simply adjust the tip-up to your desired jigging action, lower the lure and wait for a flag.

Ice anglers are also realizing the benefit of using hole cover thermal tip-ups to reduce shafts of unnatural light from penetrating the hole. Tip-up hole covers home-made from cardboard, carpet or wood can be used, or you can purchase commercially produced models.

JIGGING. Basic jigging strategies may vary from something simple as a standard bobber or slip-bobber rig, comprised of 6- to 8-pound monofilament line, split shot and a hooked minnow, to more elaborate

jigging systems involving a variety of specialized jigs and spoons.

Modern ice-fishing experts contend that during the day or times when walleyes and saugers aren't as active and must be teased into biting, modern jigging methodology is vastly superior to the standard tech-

"pounding" method as you gradually work the water column from the bottom up or as challenging as trying to trigger seemingly comatose fish.

When possible, avoid fishing clear water or shallow walleyes and saugers, especially during the day, because these daytime fish aren't as active as evening ones or fish in deep or colored water. But forced to fish in such conditions, a more aggressive, fast-moving approach is best, as this strategy doesn't allow a walleye or sauger to casually come to inspect a slow-moving bait. If they want to check out the fast-moving bait, they must strike it.

Given such conditions, ice pro Dave Genz likes to fish a Normark Jigging Rapala, or similar lure, to employ this aggressive motion. His technique involves what he describes as a snap-jigging technique, rather than a traditional lift-drop. Snap jigging is accomplished by using a relatively stiff, medium-heavy ice rod, lowering your jig to the desired depth, then snapping the rod upward with a sharp, sudden twist of the wrist and allowing the loaded stiff rod to snap the lure up.

nique of bobber-watching. A variety of equipment, lines, jigs and spoons can be used to attain quality catches, even during the day, but using a sensitive, fast-tipped, medium-heavy action ice rod, thin diameter line and specialized lures gives you the capability to work these fish efficiently, quickly sense strikes, and promote solid, immediate hook sets.

Regardless of whether you choose to use a tip-up or rod and reel, the importance of live bait can not be emphasized enough. The natural scent, consistency and taste provided by a minnow or grub help inspire more strikes and will increase your number of solid hook-ups.

PRODUCTIVE JIGGING METHODS. While jigging walleyes and saugers at night is relatively easy because most standard bobber and twitch-jigging approaches will tease fish into striking, jigging during the day is more complex. The process can be easy as packing a heavy bodied jig with maggots, lowering it, tapping the bait on bottom to attract a fish's attention, then employing an aggressive

Dave repeats this process three times, then pauses a few seconds before repeating the process. Most strikes occur on the drop or pause.

To increase your odds of making this technique work, focus your jigging along depth breaks or weedlines, drill lots of holes, and move often. The trick is turning a few neutral fish into biters and, with the odds against you, the more fish you can present your bait to, the more likely you are to trigger a few into hitting.

Heavy-bodied spoons can be used to attain similar success, and tipped with a small minnow to add natural scent and taste, their flashy, crippled minnow-imitating appearance often draws tremendous response. The addition of soft plastic, feather or hair dressings to a spoon's hook often improves the fish-attracting qualities of the lure, draw strikes to the hook, and may increase the frequency of strikes.

Most jigging spoons feature a hook attached right to the lure body. An increasing number of anglers have found that the use of a small wire clip, chain or short

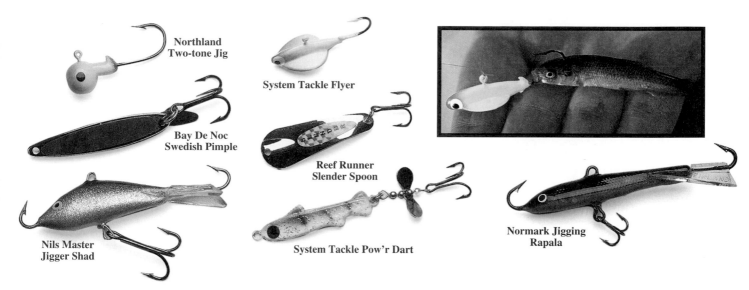

Northland Two-tone Jig

System Tackle Flyer

Bay De Noc Swedish Pimple

Reef Runner Slender Spoon

Nils Master Jigger Shad

System Tackle Pow'r Dart

Normark Jigging Rapala

HOOK a minnow through the mouth and out the top of the head when using a swimming style jig like a Flyer (inset). This method ensures the lure will work its gliding, circular action.

piece of monofilament line linking the hook to the lure body provides a distinct hooking advantage, simply because less aggressive fish can approach the hook and effortlessly suck the bait into their mouth. Just keep a needlenose pliers handy, as even short-striking fish have a tendency to swallow these dropper hooks.

Jigging minnows also work well during low-light periods. Use a simple lift of your rod tip followed by a sudden drop. The resulting slack line allows the lure to glide in a sideways, circular motion, then return. The motion attracts fish; the pause instigates most strikes.

With any of these methods, the importance of using global positioning systems (GPS) to move efficiently from structure to structure and sonar to locate specific areas and depths walleyes and saugers are holding is critical to success, as winter schools are highly mobile. As they move, you'll want to move with them, and sonar allows you to find them efficiently.

Deadsticking for Walleyes

While most walleye anglers present live minnows below a set float or slip-bobber, a few innovative fishermen have found "deadsticking" to be a simplier and better system. Deadsticking is a means of presenting live minnows without the aid of bobbers or floats. The key to the system is a custom-made 32-inch Thorne Brothers Dead Stick (right). This solid-glass ice rod features a limber tip that allows anglers to visually check the action of a minnow and detect the lightest strike. In addition, the flexible tip produces very little resistance to fish so they won't immediately drop the minnow.

To deadstick, simply set the rod in a rod holder or across the top of a bucket, lower the jig with live minnow to the bottom, then wind up enough line so the minnow hangs only a few inches off of the bottom. Close the bail on the spinning reel and watch the tip for a strike.

Since most states allow fishermen to use at least two lines during the winter season, the Dead Stick shines as a stationary rod while an angler jigs actively with another ice rod.

Yellow Perch

Yellow perch will never win any high-ranking awards for fighting ability, but they're one of the most geographically widespread and commonly caught ice-fishing species. They're also cooperative, willing winter biters, and one of the most delectable species in terms of table fare.

Yellow perch are a remarkably beautiful fish, with golden-green or grayish-brown sides accented with dark green vertical bars and bright orange or crimson-colored fins, a yellowish-white belly, and a forked tail. Yellow perch have small eyes, resulting in limited vision.

As one of the most active winter species, perch feed heavily on almost any available prey including plankton, insect larvae, crustaceans and small fish.

Habitat and Feeding Patterns

Yellow perch are a heavily schooling species that do especially well in clear, cool waters featuring hard bottoms and moderate weed growth. Shallow, vegetated bays, flats, points and humps are primary targets early and late in the season, with deep weedlines, mud flats and rocky structures producing better mid-season. Perch may flourish in shallow, densely vegetated soft-bottomed waters where they hide and feed in dense vegetation, but they also tend to overpopulate and stunt in such environments.

Most perch schools are comprised of similarly sized fish, and although winter schools are known to suspend, most feed on or near bottom. Ice anglers checking stomach contents have also noted small perch feed primarily on plankton and insect larvae, while larger fish appear to rely more on crustaceans and small minnows.

Yellow perch feed all winter, but are most likely to be caught in shallow water during first and last ice; deeper during mid-season. Due to their relatively small eyes and poor night vision, most intense feeding periods occur during the day.

WHERE TO FIND YELLOW PERCH

NATURAL LAKES. At first ice, try shallow, weedy bays, flats, bars, points and shoals featuring scattered vegetation. Densely vegetated structure will also produce, but usually only smaller fish.

During mid-season, deep holes and edges lining early-ice locations such as flats, points or bars often produce perch. On some lakes, deep, hard-bottom structure and mid-lake mud flats are also good bets.

Late in the season, deep edges lining shallow, mildly vegetated spawning bays will hold staging, pre-spawn schools, with pre-spawn fish gradually moving into shallow weedy spawning bays.

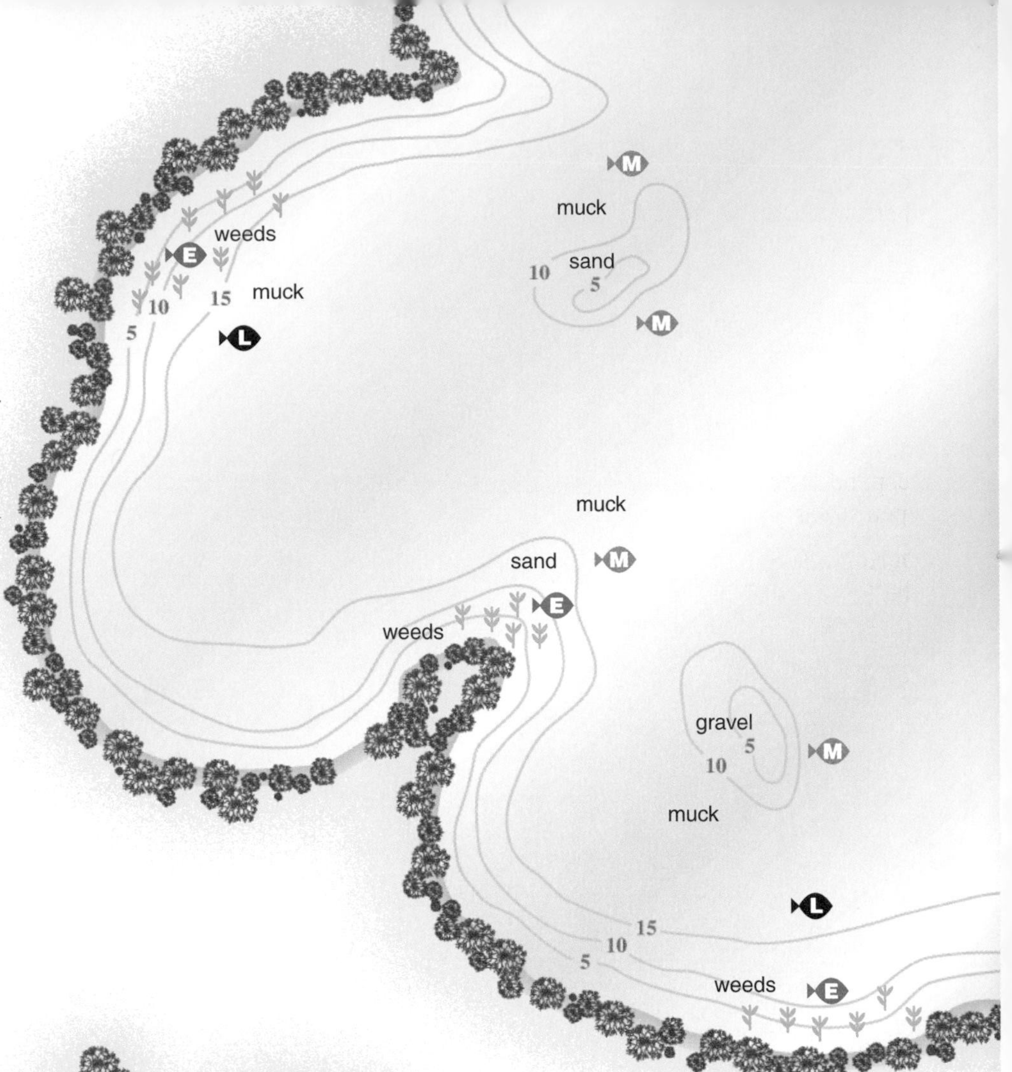

MAN-MADE LAKES. In the early season, try shallow, woody or rocky flats and shallows lining shallow, hard-bottom points and reefs.

Mid-season perch school around the base of deep, hard-bottom points and humps lining the main or secondary river channels, although soft mud flats lining these channels may produce as well.

For late season perch, try barren, sand or gravel flats just outside weedy or woody secondary creek channels fed by flowing water, where perch spawn just after ice-out.

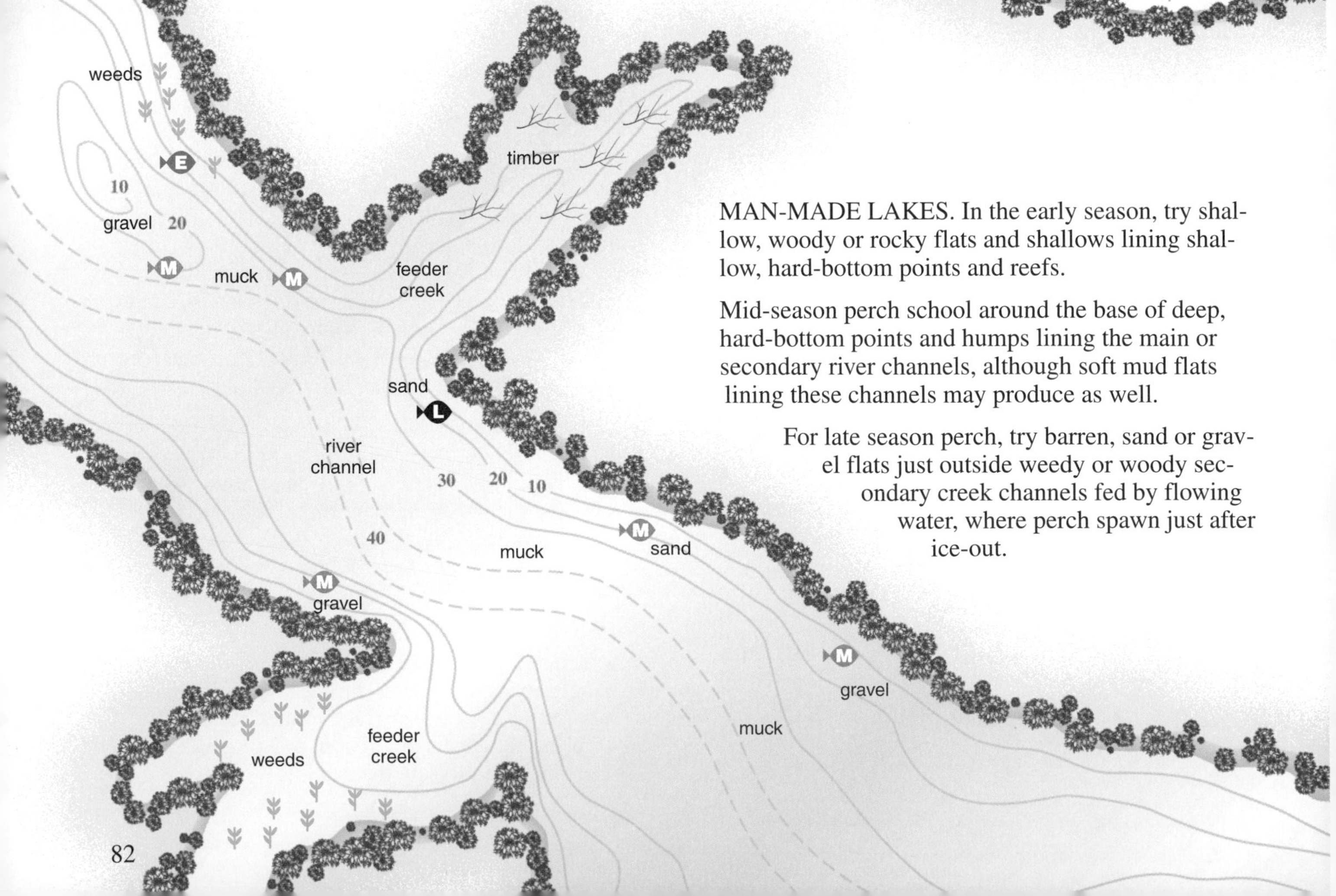

weeds
muck
sand
10   5
muck
15   muck
10
5
muck
sand
weeds
gravel
5
10
muck
15
10
5
weeds
weeds
10
gravel   20
muck
timber
feeder creek
sand
river channel
30   20   10
40
muck   sand
gravel
muck
gravel
muck
feeder creek
weeds

82

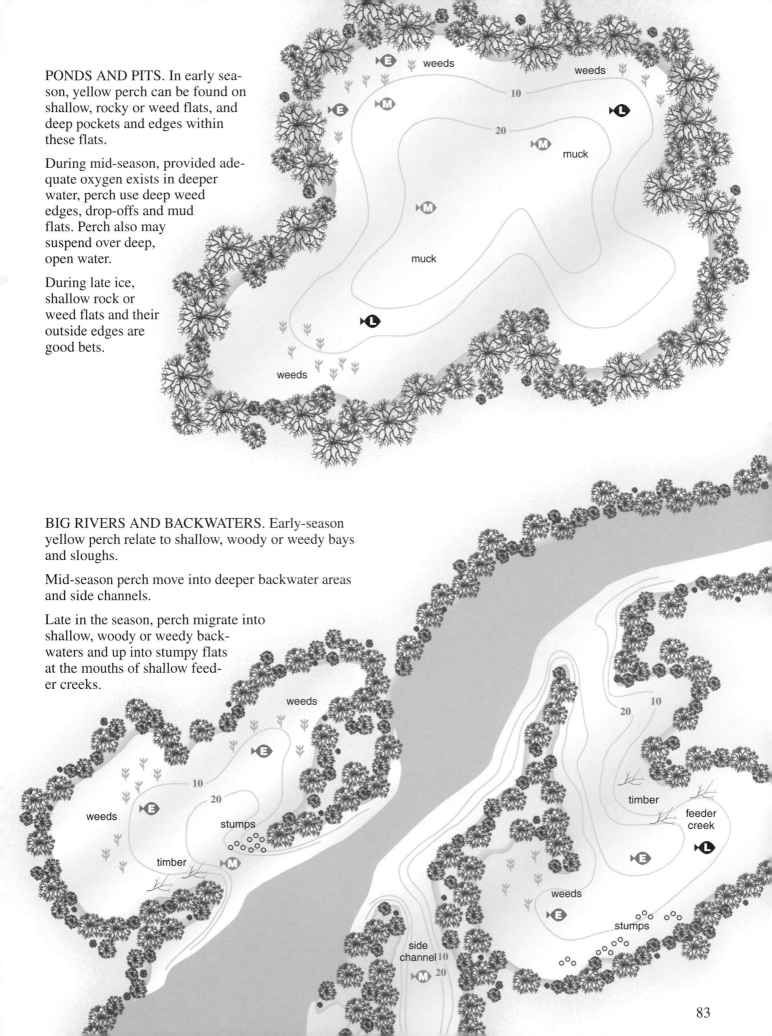

PONDS AND PITS. In early season, yellow perch can be found on shallow, rocky or weed flats, and deep pockets and edges within these flats.

During mid-season, provided adequate oxygen exists in deeper water, perch use deep weed edges, drop-offs and mud flats. Perch also may suspend over deep, open water.

During late ice, shallow rock or weed flats and their outside edges are good bets.

weeds

weeds

10

20

muck

muck

weeds

BIG RIVERS AND BACKWATERS. Early-season yellow perch relate to shallow, woody or weedy bays and sloughs.

Mid-season perch move into deeper backwater areas and side channels.

Late in the season, perch migrate into shallow, woody or weedy back-waters and up into stumpy flats at the mouths of shallow feeder creeks.

weeds

10

20

weeds

stumps

timber

10

20

timber

feeder creek

weeds

stumps

side channel 10

20

83

HOW TO CATCH YELLOW PERCH

Since yellow perch are typically aggressive winter feeders, tactics for catching them are simple. Many anglers fish tip-ups or tip-downs rigged with standard minnow rigs and, using enough split shot to place and hold the bait near bottom, hook small minnows on size 4 or 6 hooks. Colored beads, spinners or flecks of aluminum foil may also be added to create extra attraction as the bait moves.

System Tackle Genz Worm

JB Lures Hot Head

Shearwater Tackle Thumper Minnow

Ivan's Swimming Jig

Normark Jigging Rapala

Ice anglers also experience a great deal of success suspending small minnows from a small bobber fished on light line and light-action ice rods.

Since yellow perch are highly adaptive and feed on so many different types of forage, it's important to locate large perch schools with sonar, especially if the fish are suspended or schooled over deep mud flats. Next, it's important to determine what forage perch in your waters are targeting, then try to use a presentation that best emulates the preferred forage.

If the perch are feeding on insect larvae or plankton, small ice jigs tipped with grubs or maggots are the best imitators. Since perch are most likely to be feeding on or near bottom, a small-hooked, but heavy-bodied jig such as the Genz Worm or Marmooska should be used to facilitate faster, easier drops without the need for sinkers, and help hold your bait near bottom.

Given such conditions, using a small, light-hooked jig with a tiny barb or flattened barb is best, because the hook can then be cleanly inserted into the blunt end of a maggot without tearing the skin, which releases the fish attracting juices onto your fingers. Using a sharp, thin barbless or flattened-barb hook instead, these juices slowly leak out within the water, helping attract perch. Fresh bait should also be used, especially if the perch are biting light.

If yellow perch are found to be feeding on minnows, small jigs tipped with minnows can be used, but many anglers choose to use small versions of popular walleye jigs and spoons.

Where legal, many ice anglers have found the use of perch eyes or thin strips of perch belly meat horizontally rigged on a vertical or horizontal style ice jig, highly effective for triggering fussy perch. Check your local regulations before trying this technique, as some states do not allow this practice.

PRODUCTIVE JIGGING METHODS. If perch are suspended and feeding on plankton, using a basic, small-hooked but heavy bodied grub- or maggot-tipped horizontal ice jig is a good bet. Use the standard quivering sunfish-style technique, just gently wiggling the bait with a slight, gradual upward jiggling motion, followed by a slow, quivering fall. Most of the time, unlike sunfish, perch strike as the bait rises.

When perch are feeding on insect larvae or worms on deep mud flats you can use a similar tactic, but first drop your bait to the bottom, and tap it gently several times to kick up bottom sediments. This commotion attracts perch, who seemingly believing other perch have found food, attempt to move in on the action.

If the perch are found to be feeding on minnows, variations of basic walleye-style jig, spoon and jigging minnow strategies come into play. Try aggressive, pounding actions with standard jigs first. If the fish appear to be aggressive, jigging minnow-style baits like Jigging Rapalas or Flyers tipped with small minnows or a minnow head are more efficient, dropping down faster and allowing a more overall aggressive jigging approach.

Should the perch be found to not be striking readily, use of small flash spoons and walleye-style snap jigging strategies can be effective for triggering strikes. Lower your spoon to the desired depth, snap your rod upward with a sharp, sudden twist of the wrist, repeat once or twice, then pause. Strikes usually occur on the pause.

Catching Deep-Water Perch

If a school of deep-water perch isn't responding to standard winter perch strategies, try using a dropper rig to increase your chance of instigating a strike.

To make a dropper rig, remove the hook from a small perch spoon, add a short dropper leader of 4-pound monofilament and tip a plain hook or ice jig with a small minnow, waxworm or Eurolarvae. Combine a periodic, snap-jigging motion intermingled with short, finesse-style quivering. If you feel a strike, set the hook right away.

Northern Pike & Pickerel

Chain Pickerel

When many ice anglers think winter trophies, visions of huge northern pike often come to mind.

In fact, some consider northern pike and pickerel ultimate winter game. Like other popular winter species, they're found across a large portion of the north country. They have sleek, muscular bodies capable of producing fast, powerful runs, and being a cool- to cold-water loving species, are very aggressive feeders throughout the winter.

Northern pike (opposite page) feature large heads and long bodies with a white belly, elongated, pale-colored horizontal spots placed on a dark green-gold backdrop along the sides, fiery orange fins graced by black lines, and similarly colored rounded tails. While most northern pike caught through the ice weigh less than 10 pounds, some specimens tip the scales at well over 20. Measuring nearly 4 feet in length, these monstrous fish are the dreams of every ice angler that kneels down beside a tripped tip-up.

Pickerel taken through the ice are mostly chain pickerel, which rarely attain weights exceeding 4 or 5 pounds. Chain pickerel (above) feature dark, more irregularly placed, chain-like markings along pale, yellowish-green flanks.

Northern pike and pickerel are notoriously aggressive winter species, and with their commanding strength, capability to produce quick bursts of speed, large mouths, numerous sharp teeth and scalpel-sharp gill rakers, they are ruthless winter predators. If available, rounded, smooth-skinned baitfish such as shiners, smelt and cisco are preferred forage because they're easy to ingest and swallow.

Large northern pike are a tip-up fisherman's dream

HABITAT AND FEEDING PATTERNS

Northern pike and pickerel can adapt to a wide variety of environments including ponds, pits, natural and man-made lakes, rivers and river backwaters, and because they prefer cooler water temperatures, are extremely active throughout the winter months.

Moderately weedy or woody mid-depth bays, weed edges and drop-offs are common winter habitat. Green, broad-leaved vegetation and expansive stands of stumps or timber provide ample places for pike and pickerel to hide while awaiting any unaware passing baitfish.

Small pike and pickerel are most likely to hold in shallow, dense stands of weeds, and pockets within them, although pickerel attain their best growth in clear, mid-depth moderately vegetated lakes. Larger pike are often wanderers, more likely to be creatures of deep weed edges. If suspended schools of baitfish are available over deep, open water, it's not unusual for trophy pike to suspend near these food sources, roaming deep water right along with the wandering baitfish.

Northern pike and pickerel are both highly active throughout the winter months, although most fishing activity centers around the early and late ice periods, when these fish can often be found aggressively feeding in easily targeted shallow, weedy bays.

Pike bite especially well throughout the daytime hours, especially during overcast conditions, with feeding activity waning as darkness approaches.

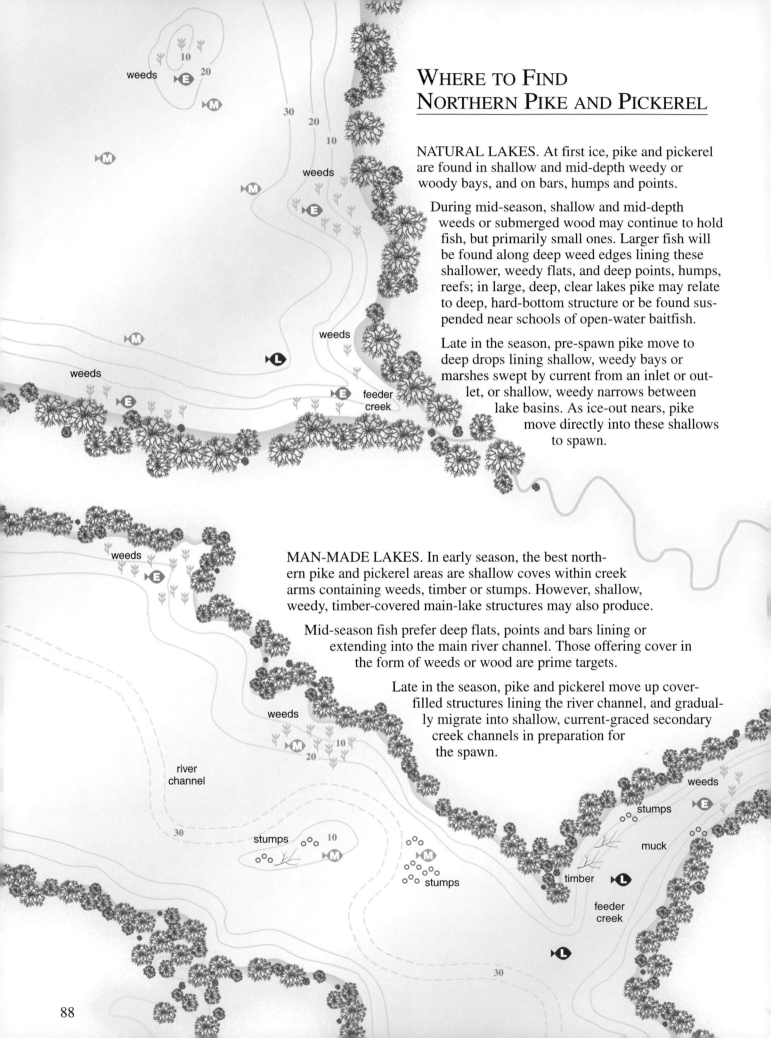

WHERE TO FIND
NORTHERN PIKE AND PICKEREL

NATURAL LAKES. At first ice, pike and pickerel are found in shallow and mid-depth weedy or woody bays, and on bars, humps and points.

During mid-season, shallow and mid-depth weeds or submerged wood may continue to hold fish, but primarily small ones. Larger fish will be found along deep weed edges lining these shallower, weedy flats, and deep points, humps, reefs; in large, deep, clear lakes pike may relate to deep, hard-bottom structure or be found suspended near schools of open-water baitfish.

Late in the season, pre-spawn pike move to deep drops lining shallow, weedy bays or marshes swept by current from an inlet or outlet, or shallow, weedy narrows between lake basins. As ice-out nears, pike move directly into these shallows to spawn.

MAN-MADE LAKES. In early season, the best northern pike and pickerel areas are shallow coves within creek arms containing weeds, timber or stumps. However, shallow, weedy, timber-covered main-lake structures may also produce.

Mid-season fish prefer deep flats, points and bars lining or extending into the main river channel. Those offering cover in the form of weeds or wood are prime targets.

Late in the season, pike and pickerel move up cover-filled structures lining the river channel, and gradually migrate into shallow, current-graced secondary creek channels in preparation for the spawn.

weeds

weeds

weeds

weeds

feeder creek

weeds

weeds

river channel

weeds

stumps

stumps

weeds

stumps

muck

timber

feeder creek

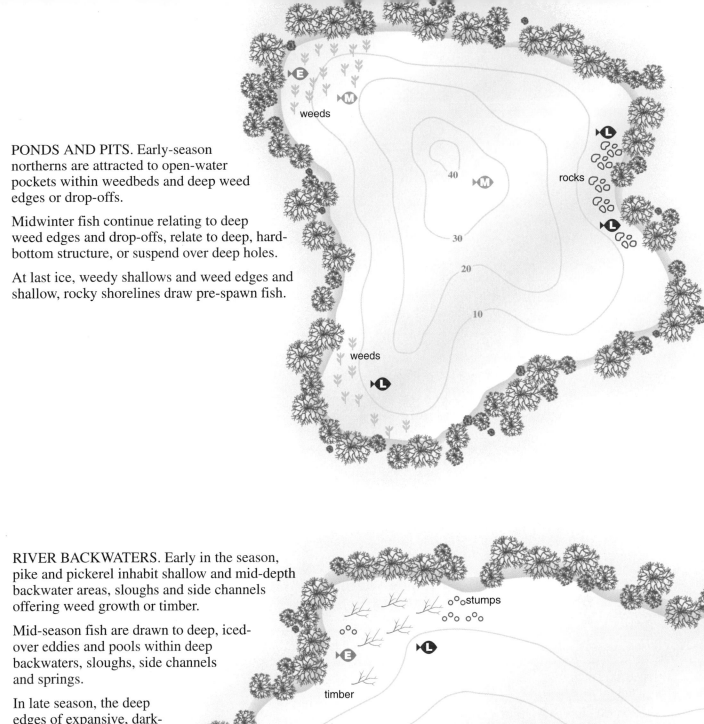

PONDS AND PITS. Early-season northerns are attracted to open-water pockets within weedbeds and deep weed edges or drop-offs.

Midwinter fish continue relating to deep weed edges and drop-offs, relate to deep, hard-bottom structure, or suspend over deep holes.

At last ice, weedy shallows and weed edges and shallow, rocky shorelines draw pre-spawn fish.

weeds

40

30

20

10

rocks

weeds

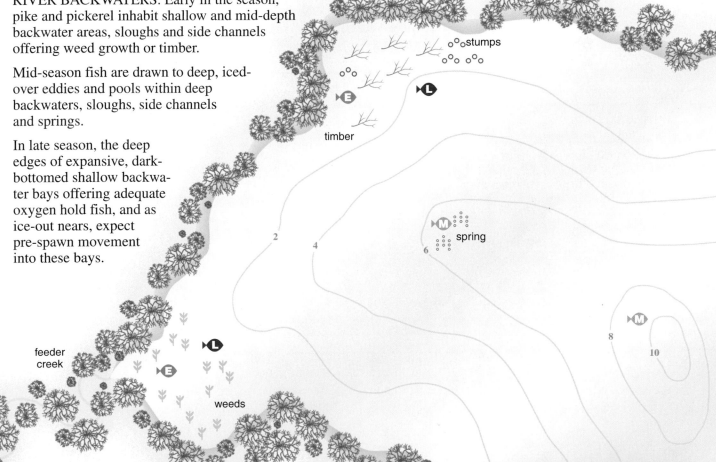

RIVER BACKWATERS. Early in the season, pike and pickerel inhabit shallow and mid-depth backwater areas, sloughs and side channels offering weed growth or timber.

Mid-season fish are drawn to deep, iced-over eddies and pools within deep backwaters, sloughs, side channels and springs.

In late season, the deep edges of expansive, dark-bottomed shallow backwater bays offering adequate oxygen hold fish, and as ice-out nears, expect pre-spawn movement into these bays.

stumps

timber

spring

2

4

6

8

10

feeder creek

weeds

PLACE tip-ups at a variety of depths along a breakline to find active northern pike. Suspend sucker or shiner minnows above the weeds to prevent fouling. In deep water, or in areas without weeds, keep the minnows near the bottom.

HOW TO CATCH
NORTHERN PIKE & PICKEREL

Unlike many other winter species, northern pike and pickerel presentations are rather simple.

TIP-UPS. Basic presentation begins with standard tip-up rigs consisting of 25-to 40-pound braided dacron line for backing, followed by a wire leader affixed with split shot and culminating with a treble-hooked minnow. A durable wire leader is important when fishing pike and pickerel, as their razor-sharp teeth and gill rakers can easily cut monofilament leaders. Most tip-up anglers agree that the use of big minnows is the ticket to bigger fish. Dead baits, especially oily, smelly baitfish

like ciscoes or smelt, appeal to the pike's acute sense of smell, and will at times draw more strikes than a live, moving presentation.

Pike and pickerel find colorful, flashy presentations highly attractive, so the use of tip-up rigs incorporating painted hooks or gaudy spinner (left) or flicker blades to add splashes of color, flash and vibration is a good idea.

To increase the attractiveness of a presentation garnished on wind activated tip-ups, a lightweight, wide-bodied flashy spoon with the hook removed can be spliced into your rig between the dacron backing and leader, with the leader then extending down to your minnow-tipped, painted hook.

Whether you choose to fish with live or dead bait, the setup used by many pike experts is the quick-strike rig (p. 37). Designed as simply a two-hook rig with meticulously razor-sharpened hooks, the front hook is merely designed to hold the rig in place on the minnow just

behind its head. The second hook, usually positioned near the dorsal fin or toward the rear of the minnow, is designed to accomplish the actual hooking.

The thinking behind such rigs is that anglers can get a fast jump on the hook set, especially with large baits, increasing hookups by reducing the number of "drops" from finicky pike. These rigs virtually eliminate problems involved with letting aggressive pike take the hooks too deep, thereby increasing the fish's chances of survival upon release.

Regardless of the type of tip-up rigging you choose to use, check it every 15 to 20 minutes to make sure the minnow hasn't been fouled by weeds. As a bonus, many times the raising and dropping of the minnow during this "weed check" tempts a neutral pike into striking.

JIGGING. Although tip-up fishing is unquestionably regarded as the most well received means of catching winter pike, jigging with bobber rigs and medium to large suckers, chubs and shiners has increased in popularity. Anglers can better control the movements of a bait with rod-and-reel, plus feel the excitement of the strike and thrill of fighting these aggressive fish on an ice rod.

elongated weedline. Use your sonar to pinpoint pockets within the vegetation or creases and turns along weed edges, then drill a number of holes through each area to facilitate complete coverage of the high-percentage edges.

Since northern pike and pickerel have such tough, bony mouths, sharpening the hooks on your jigs is of utmost importance. With a flat file this is best done by passing it along the edge of the hook point on three sides to create a strong, needle-sharp cutting point.

Pike can be caught on jigs without adding any type of bait but most ice pros recommend tipping your jigs with live or dead minnows to sweeten the offering.

POPULAR JIGGING METHODS. If northern pike and pickerel are lethargic, you can try either a plain minnow rigged on a quick-strike rig, or a light-bodied, plain jig head tipped with a tempting live minnow to initiate a take. At times, working a fast-moving, flashy spoon, vibrating bladebait or jigging minnow helps trigger strikes.

In recent years, most winter pike jigging proponents have settled on using strong, heavy-action ice rods outfitted with small baitcast or spinning reels spooled with strong lines to work a variety of jigs and spoons. They've found these systems are highly effective, and because their lines aren't set in one area, they've also found themselves more efficient in terms of increased mobility.

A great variety of jigs, spoons and bladebaits make great winter jigging lures, and a carefully positioned jigging approach is tough to top when searching for scattered pike on a large flat or along the bounds of an

With a standard jig, choose a light, flat-bodied, slow-falling design. Dressing the jig with bucktail or a hollow plastic tube design also helps slow the jig's fall. Tip the jig with a strip of minnow belly or a

Northland Air-Plane Jig

Normark Jigging Rapala

Bay De Noc Do-Jigger

whole minnow, either hooked through the lips from the bottom up to maintain a lively action with a subtle, up and down jigging motion, or try inserting the hook through the minnow's mouth, then pushing it through the top of the head and working the presentation with a gentle lift-drop motion. If desired, a more intense jigging action can be imparted to trigger fussy fish, just be sure to always keep your line taut as the jig drops and be prepared to set the hook.

Fished aggressively, swimming minnows are outstanding pike lures for fussy pike as well. Use standard lift-drop jigging motions followed by brief pauses, allowing the lure to glide widely, then rest, but don't allow the lure to remain still for long. Although most strikes can be anticipated during the brief pause, some pike will strike the moving lure, so be sure to follow the slack line with your rod and always be prepared to set the hook.

For active fish, try using a heavy-bodied, tight-wiggling spoon or bladebait, and work it aggressively. Known as "rip-jigging," this technique involves use of periodic, aggressive upward snaps of the wrist followed by a gentle, wiggling motion on the downward fall. When "ripped" in such fashion, a stiff, heavy-action rod brings an immediate, quick upward movement of the lure, followed up by a slow, sudden falling, wiggling bait. While fussy pike can be triggered by the ripping motion itself, they usually strike immediately after the quick upward motion, just as the lure begins to fall. Aggressive fish may strike at any time.

In the event you find pike active, virtually any flashy, heavy-bodied jig, bladebait or spoon that gets to the depth of the pike quickly and can be aggressively jigged will draw smashing strikes unparalled by any other winter species.

Accessing Trophy Pike

While northern pike grow to trophy proportions throughout much of Canada, most of these hotspots are difficult, even dangerous, to reach during the ice-fishing season. Many trophy pike hunters, however, have found the perfect combination of safe ice and big fish in Buffalo Bay and Muskeg Bay of Lake of the Woods.

Located along the Manitoba—Minnesota border, these two massive bays give anglers an excellent chance at a 20-pound pike. Prime pike locations include underwater points and inside turns, shallow bars, rock reefs, and flats adjacent to river mouths.

Most trophy pike are caught in relatively shallow water, usually from 5 to 10 feet deep, on tip-ups rigged with deadbaits. To ensure successful catch and release on these big fish, quick-strike rigs are the obvious choice.

Buffalo Bay and Muskeg Bay pike fishing is good throughout the entire winter season with the number-one trophy-producing month being March.

Anglers wanting up to the minute information on ice and fishing conditions in the area can call Buffalo Bay Resort at 204-437-2402.

Lake Trout & Splake

In ice-fishing legacies, few fish carry the aura of a giant lake trout. The chance of icing a giant laker weighing 10, 20, or 30 or more pounds is enough to lure anglers onto ice covering water depths in excess of a couple hundred feet. And being a slow-growing, monstrous trophy fish, most anglers consider the pursuit of these giants great adventure.

Within ice-fishing realms, the lake trout's faster growing, but usually smaller, hybridized offspring—the splake—is commonly mistaken for a laker. These two fish are best distinguished in two ways: side markings and tail shape.

Lake trout (right) feature a spattering of pale, cream-colored markings on a greenish-gray or dark brownish-black, and feature a characteristically distinct, deeply forked tail, while splake (below) have light spots on their sides, peanut-shaped markings on top and a more rounded tail.

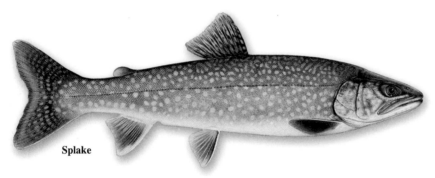

Splake

While lake trout and splake may suspend, both are cold, deep-water, bottom-loving species. Due to the lack of light within their preferred immense depths, they have sharply developed eyes, noses and lateral lines. Forage may consist of insect larvae, worms, crustaceans and deep-water forage fish such as ciscoes, suckers, whitefish and smelt.

HABITAT AND FEEDING PATTERNS

Lake trout and splake are limited in distribution to the deep, cold, well-oxygenated waters of the Canadian Shield and Great Lakes, natural lakes and deep mine pits of the north-central and northeast United States and high elevation mountain lakes of western North America.

Within deep, sterile Canadian Shield and mountain lakes or icy Great Lakes bays where water temperature and oxygen remain sufficient, frozen river mouths, narrows between lake basins, narrows separating lakes or steep breaks lining rocky islands all hold forage and are good fishing locations. Shallow and mid-depth reefs, points and humps may also be productive.

On deep inland lakes or mine pits supporting lakers and splake, the same areas will often produce, but mid-depth and deep points, humps and walls are primary locations. Both species may also suspend in such environments.

Deep-water lake trout and splake feed best during the bright light of day, presumably when they can see best. Shallow-water fish are primarily twilight feeders.

Lake trout on a rocky reef

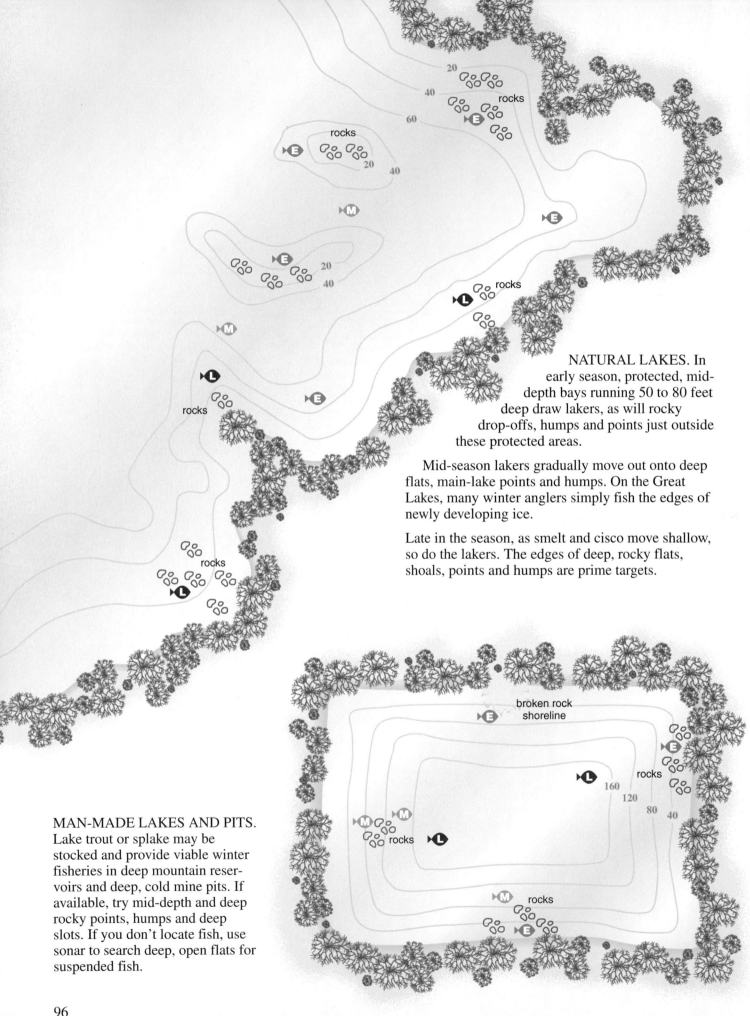

NATURAL LAKES. In early season, protected, mid-depth bays running 50 to 80 feet deep draw lakers, as will rocky drop-offs, humps and points just outside these protected areas.

Mid-season lakers gradually move out onto deep flats, main-lake points and humps. On the Great Lakes, many winter anglers simply fish the edges of newly developing ice.

Late in the season, as smelt and cisco move shallow, so do the lakers. The edges of deep, rocky flats, shoals, points and humps are prime targets.

MAN-MADE LAKES AND PITS. Lake trout or splake may be stocked and provide viable winter fisheries in deep mountain reservoirs and deep, cold mine pits. If available, try mid-depth and deep rocky points, humps and deep slots. If you don't locate fish, use sonar to search deep, open flats for suspended fish.

HOW TO CATCH LAKE TROUT AND SPLAKE

Basic tip-up rigs for lake trout and splake consist of simple hook and minnow rigs on large-spooled tip-ups such HT's deep lake Polar or Fisherman tip-ups made to hold lots of line for accessing deep water. The most popular rig consists of dacron line, a length of heavy mono or "superline" leader set with a heavy egg or bass bullet-sinker rigged as a slip-weight to drop the bait to bottom and hold it there, yet still allows a fish to run and eventually trip a tip-up flag. Lakers and splake will hit live or dead smelt, cisco or suckers, but check the local regulations for the waters you plan to fish.

Historically, deep lake trout jigging equipment consisted of a basic bobbing stick, essentially a sanded, hand-held block of wood cut with a hole to provide a comfortable hold for the angler and smoothed ends to accommodate wraps of dacron. This line was rigged with a heavily weighted bait or lure, which was lowered to bottom and jigged. Amazingly, such traditional lines are still in use today.

Modern ice anglers, however, use live or dead bait rigs fished on heavy-action rod and reel combos, spooled with 25- to 30-pound dacron or Spectra-braided superlines. Some anglers, however, opt for specialized rods with roller tips and guides designed for wire lines. Spectra and wire both feature very little stretch allowing for improved hook sets, but most ice anglers appreciate Spectra because its thin diameter slices down fast and stays deep, even in current.

The dacron, Spectra or wire is then rigged to a three-way swivel, outfitted with a heavy egg sinker often weighing ¾ ounce or larger on the drop-line, and a short leader tipped with a hooked smelt or strip of minnow belly from a cisco, smelt or sucker.

While the three-way swivel rig is very effective, many lake trout anglers prefer to fish with jigs. Due to the tremendous depths most lake trout are found, large, heavy jigs weighing ¾ of an ounce or more are usually needed. In very deep water with strong currents, jigs weighing 1 to 3 ounces are necessary to reach and stay near the bottom. If lake trout are striking short, stinger hooks may be added to the jigs to improve hooking.

When deep-water currents aren't strong, jigging with smaller, ½- to ¾-ounce jigs or large, heavy, flashy jigging spoons and vibrating bladebaits attract lakers. Such baits can be jigged using a moderate lift-drop action within a foot of bottom or an aggressive snap-jigging motion, but typically a mixture of the two methods, meaning a moderate lift-drop timed with periodic snap-jigging motions, results in the most strikes.

Winged swimming jigs, often called *airplane jigs*, are favorites of many winter lake trout anglers because they allow you to cover lots of water. When lifted and dropped, airplane jigs glide to the side in wide, circular motions to cover water while creating fish-attracting movement.

Cut bait is commonly used to dress jigs, and while there's really no science to this practice, it is important to make sure the dressing complements your lure's action rather than impede it.

Some anglers cut strips of minnow belly from just in front of the fins to the tail, or long, slender slices from the minnow's side. Many believe tapering these strips from front to back adds a more realistic swimming motion. Otherwise, try tapering the strips on each side, and hooking them in the middle, creating an undulating, "V-shaped" strip.

Northland Air-plane Jig

Northland Sting'r Bucktail Jig

Berkley Power Pro Tube

Ivan's Slammer

Stream Trout

S tream trout are typically made available to ice anglers through the stocking of deep, cold natural and man-made lakes, ponds and pits.

The attraction of stream trout is easy to understand, as they are unquestionably among the most beautifully marked of all winter species, typically bite cooperatively, especially during early and late in the winter, fight well, and their tasty, flakey fillets are the envy of even the fussiest gourmet chefs.

A number of stream trout species may be taken through the ice, but catches primarily consist of rainbow, brown, brook and cutthroat trout.

Rainbows are easy to identify by their silvery iridescent sides split by a distinctive, pink line and random, black dots splattered across their sides and tail.

Brown trout are usually darker, with light brownish-yellow sides marked with black, orange and reddish spots.

Brook trout are perhaps the most colorful of the winter stream trout. Light, wormlike markings on their backs give way to pale green sides marked with light red, blue and crimson spots, and light crimson reddish-orange fins lined by black and white borders.

Cutthroat feature a rainbow trout-like pink stripe on their flanks, garnished with black specks cast on a greenish yellow backdrop. Their name is derived from the distinct, crimson red streaks on the underside of their gills.

Fisherman icing a big rainbow

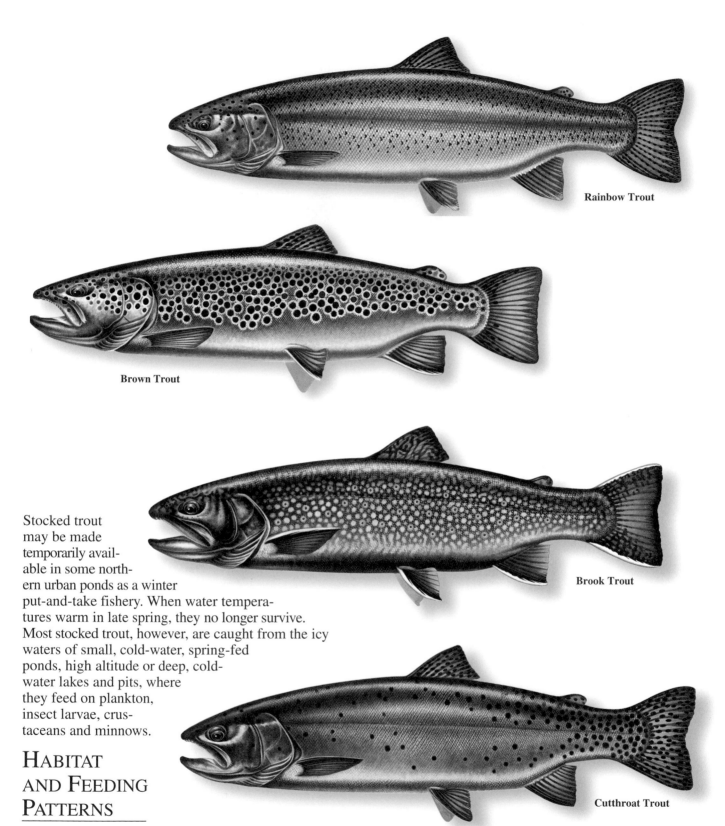

Rainbow Trout

Brown Trout

Brook Trout

Cutthroat Trout

Stocked trout may be made temporarily available in some northern urban ponds as a winter put-and-take fishery. When water temperatures warm in late spring, they no longer survive. Most stocked trout, however, are caught from the icy waters of small, cold-water, spring-fed ponds, high altitude or deep, cold-water lakes and pits, where they feed on plankton, insect larvae, crustaceans and minnows.

HABITAT AND FEEDING PATTERNS

Stocked stream trout thrive in a variety of cold-water lakes, ranging from spring-fed farm ponds to the vast Great Lakes. Gradually sloping shorelines and points offering weeds, wood or broken rock hold forage and will all attract stocked stream trout, although these fish are especially attracted to current-graced springs, inlets and outlets. Stream trout are also known to suspend over deep, open water. Fishing action is typically best early and late in the season.

Although stream trout may bite throughout the day, ice anglers often find the best action during the low-light periods of early morning or late afternoon.

WHERE TO FIND STREAM TROUT

NATURAL LAKES. At first ice, stream trout are often caught near the mouths of incoming feeder creeks, and on slow-tapering shallow flats, humps and points.

Mid-season trout inhabit these same areas, but most species are prone to suspending over deep water.

Late in the hard-water season, some stream trout continue to suspend, although shallow, forage-rich bays, inlet and outlet areas become increasingly productive.

TWO-STORY LAKES. Deep, natural lakes featuring enough cold water in the depths to maintain adequate conditions to support a year-round trout fishery are known as "two-story" lakes, with warm-water species inhabiting the warmer bays and the trout holding deep. Even though winter temperatures allow trout to move freely, most fish continue holding on deep, main-lake structure and along steep drops lining the main-lake basin throughout the winter, rather than compete with other warm-water species in shallower bays and flats.

MAN-MADE LAKES. Most man-made lakes aren't deep and cold enough to support stocked trout, but some Canadian Shield, high-elevation mountain and deep prairie reservoirs may provide suitable cold-water environments.

In the early season, trout relate to deep shoreline structure, particularly points and incoming stream mouths, cold-water intakes or cold-water outflows.

During mid-season, trout often suspend near the steep breaks along deep shoreline structure such as points and humps.

Late-season trout are drawn to shallow and mid-depth flats and shoreline structure, especially spots located near inlets or outlets.

PONDS AND PITS. At first ice, trout can be caught on shallow, forage-rich flats and structures featuring weeds, wood or broken rock.

By mid-season, most fish suspend over deep structure or deep, open water.

Late in the season, look for trout on shallow, forage-rich flats and structures featuring weeds, wood or broken rock and the edges where these features break into deeper water.

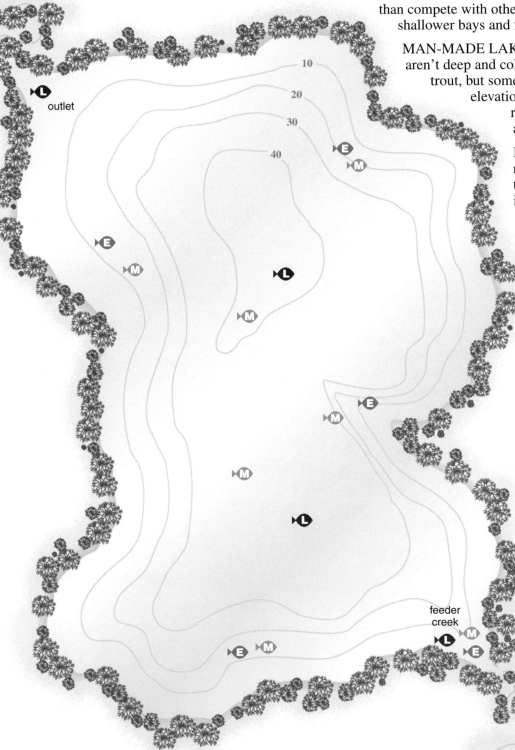

Angler holding a beautifully marked brook trout

HOW TO CATCH STREAM TROUT

Most winter anglers enjoy the special thrill of jigging for stocked trout, but some enjoy success on tip-ups, too. Long, light monofilament leaders rigged with tiny ultralight shot and small hooks tipped with insect larvae, grubs, small minnows, or even corn, creating natural slow-drop offerings are standard riggings. Change the depth of your presentation periodically to help find the primary strike zone.

Since stocked trout are very mobile and may hold directly on bottom or suspend, the use of sonar to help find them is important. Once found, trout in shallow or mid-depth natural lakes, ponds and Great Lakes bays can easily be fished with medium-action ice rods and reels and grub-tipped hooks or teardrop jigs. For increased sport, however, many trout experts are switching to light- and ultralight-action ice rods, light lines and a variety of vertical or horizontal-style ice jigs.

Small spoons rigged with dropper lines tied to small maggot- or insect larvae-tipped hooks or wet flies are also popular with many winter trout enthusiasts. The flash helps attract fish from a distance, and the dropper line often triggers them into striking.

In deep Great Lakes areas, deep reservoirs, pits and high-elevation trout lakes, stout rods and heavy lines are usually employed. The stiff-action rod and heavy line allows for firm, solid hook-sets and fighting power when targeting trout in deep water.

To complement these deep-water spinning or bait-casting outfits, most anglers prefer heavyweight jigs and lures to help drop their presentations fast, then hold them at the desired depth. Large grubs such as mealworms or small minnows are typically the baits of choice.

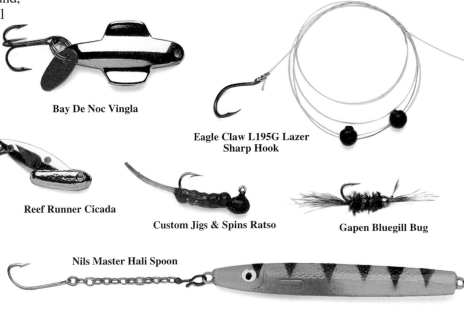

Bay De Noc Vingla

Reef Runner Cicada

Eagle Claw L195G Lazer Sharp Hook

Custom Jigs & Spins Ratso

Gapen Bluegill Bug

Nils Master Hali Spoon

Salmon

Salmon are historically a river species successfully stocked in some large, deep, cold lakes—and a few exclusive, adventuresome ice anglers have learned that where these lakes freeze, salmon are fair game.

Without question, it's the aggressive strikes and hard-fighting power of these fish that attracts most winter anglers; coho and chinook salmon have been known to fight 30 minutes or longer beneath the ice. Furthermore, few will argue the table fare of a salmon steak baked, grilled or smoked to perfection.

Due to the salmon's strict requirements for deep, cold water, their distribution and availability to ice anglers is geographically limited; and because they are a nomadic, roaming species often searching for open-water schools of baitfish, finding and catching them is no easy task. But once hooked, these powerful fish are a challenge for even the most skilled winter angler.

Several species may be taken through the ice, but kokanee, landlocked, coho and chinook are the most commonly caught species.

Kokanee salmon, a freshwater derivative of the sockeye salmon, have been stocked in some deep, cold lakes and reservoirs of the western United States and Canada. While small and slim, they are muscular, hard-fighting fish that can be identified by their arctic bluish-green back and, unlike their closely related cousin the sockeye, have no black spots on their tails. They feed on plankton and small minnows.

Landlocked salmon, a freshwater form of the Atlantic salmon, have

Landlocked salmon taken on a tip-up

been successfully stocked in several deep, cold lakes in the northeastern United States and eastern Canada. This well-respected, hard-fighting fish at times is mistaken for brown trout, because of their large, dark spots encircled by light colored rings. They feed mainly on minnows.

Kokanee Salmon

Coho salmon are primarily caught along frozen Great Lakes bays. These extremely powerful, voracious fish are best identified by their white gums. Being large predators, they feed almost exclusively on forage fish such as alewives and smelt.

Like the coho, chinook salmon are primarily available in frozen Great Lakes bays, but successful plantings have been established in some deep, cold inland lakes such as South Dakota's Lake Oahe and North Dakota's Lake Sakakawea. These strong, hard-running fish are best identified by their black gums. Chinook feed on baitfish such as alewives and smelt.

Landlocked Salmon

HABITAT AND FEEDING PATTERNS

Being a nomadic species, structure and cover aren't as important to salmon as most winter species. Instead, they relate mostly to food supply. This makes consistent winter catches difficult, and even the best winter angler will admit that action is seldom fast-paced. Still, some anglers think winter salmon don't move as much as once believed, and while waits between fish can be long, the chance of hooking into one of these exceptionally strong fighting, powerful running fish makes all the work and wait worthwhile.

Coho Salmon

Most salmon activity is confined to the low-light periods of early morning and late afternoon, but the duration of these feeding periods may extend into midmorning and begin again by midafternoon.

Chinook Salmon

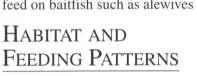

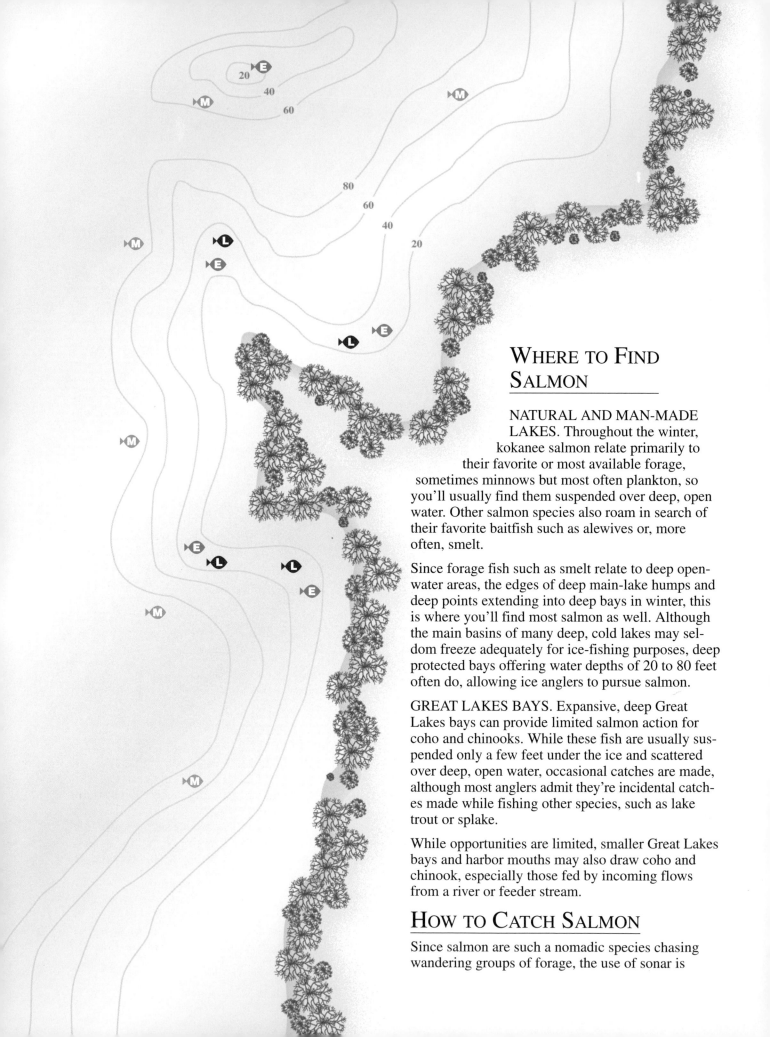

WHERE TO FIND SALMON

NATURAL AND MAN-MADE
LAKES. Throughout the winter,
kokanee salmon relate primarily to
their favorite or most available forage,
sometimes minnows but most often plankton, so
you'll usually find them suspended over deep, open
water. Other salmon species also roam in search of
their favorite baitfish such as alewives or, more
often, smelt.

Since forage fish such as smelt relate to deep open-
water areas, the edges of deep main-lake humps and
deep points extending into deep bays in winter, this
is where you'll find most salmon as well. Although
the main basins of many deep, cold lakes may seldom freeze adequately for ice-fishing purposes, deep
protected bays offering water depths of 20 to 80 feet
often do, allowing ice anglers to pursue salmon.

GREAT LAKES BAYS. Expansive, deep Great
Lakes bays can provide limited salmon action for
coho and chinooks. While these fish are usually suspended only a few feet under the ice and scattered
over deep, open water, occasional catches are made,
although most anglers admit they're incidental catches made while fishing other species, such as lake
trout or splake.

While opportunities are limited, smaller Great Lakes
bays and harbor mouths may also draw coho and
chinook, especially those fed by incoming flows
from a river or feeder stream.

HOW TO CATCH SALMON

Since salmon are such a nomadic species chasing
wandering groups of forage, the use of sonar is

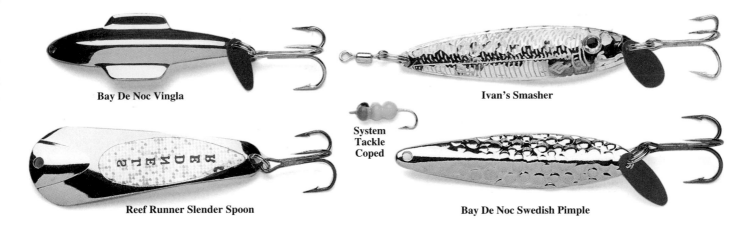

Bay De Noc Vingla

Ivan's Smasher

Reef Runner Slender Spoon

System Tackle Coped

Bay De Noc Swedish Pimple

imperative to locating them with any degree of consistency. A good plan is to use sonar to identify suspended schools of baitfish such as smelt or cisco, then look for larger marks indicating the presence of suspended salmon, usually found holding at the same depth or just beneath the forage. You should also prepare to drill numerous holes while searching for active fish.

If by chance a school of fish is found, which may happen in some large reservoirs, crowds of ice anglers can quickly develop. If so, try fishing the outside edges of the group to increase your chance of presenting your bait to the "freshest" fish in the school. And if fishing slows in a specific area, move to find another school. Some ice experts feel schools of salmon in deep reservoirs congregate in certain areas at the beginning of winter and don't move far, which explains why once a school has been fished down, action often slows for the remainder of the winter season.

Should you plan to fish with live bait, you can use the smelt tactics (p. 110) or tullibee techniques (p. 107) identified in the smelt and tullibee segments of this book to catch your own natural live bait. The use of natural forage has been found to make significant improvements in winter salmon catches. Just be sure such practices are legal. In most states, transport of live smelt is illegal, but it's okay to use live smelt, provided you can catch them on-site. Other states don't allow use of live smelt for salmon at all. Check your local regulations.

TIP-UPS. Many salmon are caught by anglers using large-spooled underwater tip-ups, which hold tremendous quantities of line. Not only are these long lines needed to reach the depths salmon often suspend, but more importantly, to provide ample backing for these hard-fighting, hard-running fish. Dacron backing followed by long lengths of either heavy monofilament, Spectra or even thin wire line rigged with a live or dead smelt hung just below schools of forage fish account for the most strikes.

When conditions allow, large-spooled wind tip-ups rigged with minnow-tipped spoons can also be highly effective.

JIGGING. The most basic jigging presentation for salmon involves use of sturdy, heavy-action ice rods outfitted with either a good quality baitcasting or spinning reel. Spooled with 8- to 12-pound monofilament line and rigged with a live, nose-hooked shiner or smelt dangled beneath a slip bobber, you can precisely set your line to deliver the bait just below the school of forage fish.

Perhaps the most popular way to fish winter salmon is to use a sturdy, medium-heavy-action ice rod combo and 6- to 12-pound monofilament line rigged with flashy jigging spoons tipped with a piece of cut smelt. Color can be important and should be experimented with, but many winter salmon experts believe the brighter, shinier and cleaner the spoon's finish, the better it works. To keep your spoon's finish attractive and shiny, use a sparkling glass cleaner and chamois cloth to polish the finish to a glaring, bright shine.

Rather than tying a snap-swivel directly to the spoon, splice a ball-bearing swivel about 18 inches up the line from the spoon's split ring. This way, you can prevent line twist otherwise common with fluttering jigging spoons.

To fish with a jigging spoon, lower it to the base of the school of smelt, and begin an aggressive, snap-jigging approach, occasionally dropping it to flutter down a few feet below the school. Most strikes occur on these downward falls, because salmon instinctively strike the spoon, thinking they're nailing a hapless, injured baitfish dropping from the school.

For the smaller, plankton-feeding kokanee salmon, a more delicate presentation is necessary. For most applications, a medium-action spinning rod rigged with a spring bobber, 2- to 6-pound line and a small, plankton-imitating ice jig like the System Tackle Coped works nicely.

Tullibee

As ice fishing has developed into a major participant sport, the interest in various species has boomed—particularly for unique fish such as tullibee. Although they don't grow large, they can attain weights of up to 5 pounds. They're great sport on light tackle, and many anglers compare the taste of smoked tullibee to trout or salmon.

Tullibee, otherwise known as cisco, are often referred to as "lake herring," a tradition brought by early Swede and Finnish immigrants familiar with saltwater herring in their homelands. Tullibee can be identified by their iridescent, silvery sides, small mouths and forked tails.

With their small mouths, tullibee feed primarily on plankton, insect larvae and tiny minnows. They prefer the deep, cold environments of large oligotrophic lakes, but can be found in virtually any clear, cool-water lake offering at least a section of deep, cold water throughout the year. They usually school tightly, and anglers locating a group of fish often catch one after another for an entire afternoon.

During early and mid-season, tullibee are a wandering species that can be found suspended virtually anywhere in deep, open water, but usually 20 to 50 feet down from the surface, with depth changes common. By late winter, they'll group on shallow flats and feed actively.

Tullibee feed heavily from late morning to early afternoon. Action usually subsides by late afternoon.

How to Catch Tullibee

Since tullibee typically cruise through deep, open water and suspend, sonar is critical to finding fish and the specific depth they're feeding.

Traditionally, anglers used stiff jig poles spooled with dacron line attached to spoons and 4- to 6-pound monofilament dropper lines leading to ice jigs tipped with small minnows or mayfly larvae. In recent years, however, many anglers have opted for light to medium-light-action spinning combos

spooled with 2- to 4-pound monofilament line. These combos are much more user friendly for rigging slip-bobbers and small hooks tipped with either small minnows or mayfly larvae, or traditional dropper spoon setups. Most winter tullibee anglers drill a series of two or three evenly spaced holes and, depending on local regulations, fish either one or two slip-bobber lines while jigging with a small spoon and dropper line.

Many winter anglers believe the first silver-spoon dropper rigs were developed by winter tullibee anglers, and for good reason: the weight of the spoon allows the presentation to be lowered quickly to deep, suspended fish, and the lure's silvery flash simulates the feeding activity of other cisco. About the time a cisco moves in to investigate, the tiny, bait-tipped ice jig appears, initiating strikes.

Winter tullibee often feed on insect larvae and nymphs, specifically mayfly nymphs (below). Although sold in some bait shops as wigglers, mayflies can be hard to obtain and, since they must be kept in water, are difficult to conveniently transport on the ice. To offset this situation, experienced winter tullibee anglers often cut open the stomachs of caught tullibee and remove mayflies from their bellies for use as bait.

This might sound strange, but tullibee will strike even dead mayfly nymphs, and during late ice when mayfly nymphs are most abundant, tullibee eat so many of these little bugs, it's not unusual to find them swallowed whole and still alive in a tullibee's stomach, providing a convenient source of bait.

Whitefish

Whitefish are found only in select, deep cold-water lakes, and while they may suspend to feed on small baitfish, whitefish are primarily bottom feeders, preying mostly on tiny minnows or invertebrates such as freshwater shrimp, snails or insect larvae. The whitefish's popularity is highly regionalized, but they do have a following along the Great Lakes and throughout eastern Canada. They are also known for their quality table fare.

Whitefish can be identified by their silvery white sides, copper brown top sections and orangish-colored anal fin.

The best time to catch winter whitefish is early ice (November or early December), when straggling, late spawning or post-spawn whitefish are still congregated along 15- to 20-foot shoreline flats and bays. Small, shaded, wind-protected bays afford the best first-ice action, simply because they're first to freeze.

During mid-season, schools of post-spawn whitefish often move along points leading from these shoreline flats and bays toward the main-lake basin. The fish often hold along steep breaking broken rock fingers and outside turns along the edges of the most prominent, hard-bottom main-lake points before scattering along deep, main-lake drop-offs and mud flats, where they become difficult to find and catch consistently. Late in the winter, whitefish loosely group around the bases of deep, main-lake points.

Whitefish are most active during the low-light conditions of mid- to late afternoon, although early morning hours can be productive as well.

HOW TO CATCH WHITEFISH

The best time to approach whitefish is during first ice, but since the ice is typically clear and seldom covered by snow at this point, whitefish are likely to spook as you walk out and drill holes. However, whitefish will return within a half hour if you sit quietly. Try drilling a number of holes up and down the structure you intend to fish, then use a blanket, piece of carpeting, or sit inside a mobile fish shelter to shade your presence, and sit quietly and wait for them to return.

Most anglers fish in groups and, because whitefish are opportunistic bottom feeders, often scatter standard underwater tip-ups set with two- or four-arm wire spreader rigs (below) across the bottom of a breaking point. Anglers then fish with tiny ice jigs tipped with waxworms, salmon roe or small minnows in holes somewhere in between. The tip-ups not only help improve whitefish catches, but help indicate when whitefish are moving, and where.

To attract whitefish, some winter anglers have found sparing use of oatmeal an effective means of chumming. As the oatmeal absorbs water and sinks, whitefish move in. Just don't use much. Feeding whitefish may gorge themselves on the oatmeal, and as the oatmeal absorbs water and expands, it can bloat their stomachs, killing fish.

Other anglers chum with whitefish eggs stripped from ripe females that have been caught and kept. These eggs also work well when placed on the hooks of tiny ice jigs.

Spreader Rigs

In southern Ontario, the standard method for fishing whitefish involves use of a permanent shanty—or "hut" as locals call them—and special balance tip-downs rigged with dacron line and bottom set double wire spreader rigs tipped with two small hooks baited with tiny minnows. Anglers usually drop dead minnows with their air bladders popped down the holes to attract whitefish, and simply tap the arm periodically to create a fish-attracting bottom disturbance.

Wire spreader rigs are good presentation tools because they allow you to fish bait directly on bottom, yet keep the minnows spread apart. While both two- and four-arm wire spreader rigs are commercially purchased, many veteran whitefish anglers make their own.

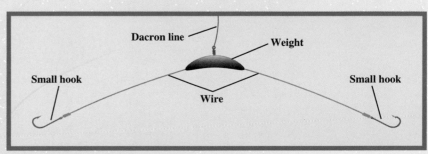

Smelt

With smelt not as widely distributed as many winter species and the average catch measuring only 6 inches in length, many anglers are surprised to find crowds gathered on the ice pursuing these silvery little flecks. But these crowds know a secret: what these fish lack in size, they make up for in flavor. Smelt are a small, thin, iridescent silvery-flanked fish with small, toothy mouths. They feed on insect larvae, small worms, tiny crustaceans and small fish within the frozen waters of the Great Lakes, Lake Champlain and some small lakes throughout the northeast United States. Smelt also inhabit estuaries lining the east coast of North America, and a few geographically isolated lakes throughout North American ice-fishing climes where they've been stocked as supplemental forage bases for larger gamefish.

In small, shallow waters where smelt have been stocked as forage, expect early-season schools to suspend over the deepest available water. Late-season smelt may move toward inlet mouths where they stage before making their upstream spawning runs.

In large, deep, cold lakes, early-season smelt usually suspend over deep, open water. It's not uncommon to find schools holding at depths of 30 to 80 feet or more. By late ice, they'll shift toward inlet mouths prior to their spring spawning runs. In the large, deep lakes of the northeast and Great Lakes bays, late-ice smelt concentrate heavily and are caught in huge numbers.

In Atlantic estuaries, smelt often school in large, ice-coated eddies, where they can be caught during tidal movements, especially in early and late winter. At last ice, they may congregate near feeder creeks and inlets adjoining these eddies.

Smelt usually bite best after dark or during low-light periods when they tend to move higher in the water column and become more active. Some anglers even use lanterns to draw these schools higher, where they're more easily accessible. In estuaries of the east coast, the best action occurs during the rising or falling tide, when water movement stirs forage.

HOW TO CATCH SMELT

Since schools of smelt are often deep-water roamers and schools may pass through quickly, dropping your bait down to the proper depth, hooking your fish, retrieving it and returning your bait back to the school has to be fast. To accommodate these needs, devout winter deep-water smelt anglers in the northeastern United States have devised special smelt rig lines (below).

Jigging for smelt is popular in shallow, coastal estuaries or during late ice when smelt are shallower and most easily accessible. Small jig rods tipped with spring bobbers or light-action ice combos are most frequently used, and tiny grub or minnow-hooked jigs and teardrops are mandatory in order to consistently hook these small-mouthed fish. Small, silvery spoons tipped with dropper lines leading to small-hooked jigs are also effective. In Atlantic estuaries, small seaworms or bits of cut seaworms are effectively used as jig tippers.

During early and midwinter, rod and reel anglers often catch deep-water smelt with in-line tube rigs or other heavy weights to efficiently drop tiny lures and baits into the depths. Egg shells may also be used as chum to attract wandering schools of deep-water smelt.

Another trick used by long-time winter smelt anglers is to tie a small hook with bits of yarn and then dip it in iodine. The iodine smells much like a seaworm, and when smelt strike, the yarn gets tangled in their tiny teeth, allowing a better hook set. This technique is especially effective in saltwater estuaries where smelt commonly feed on seaworms.

How to Make and Use a Speed Reel

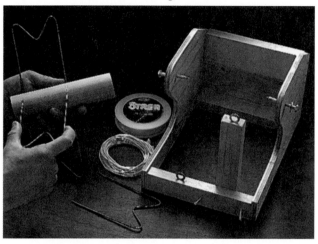

1. FORCE wire line holders into holes drilled in a 1½-inch wooden dowel. Seat the dowel in the frame so it turns freely. Wind 100 feet of 6-pound mono on the line holders and 25 feet of cord on the dowel. Run the line and cord through small screw eyes.

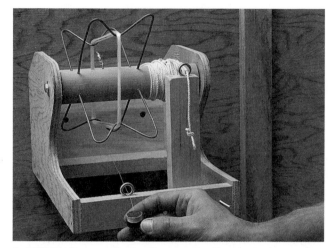

2. THREAD a small slip-float on the line and add a tandem hook rig with #10 hooks. Do not peg the float to the line or attach a bobber stop. Bait with 1- to 1½-inch shiner minnows hooked through the lips. Lower the rig to the desired depth.

3. EXPERIMENT with different depths until you find the smelt. Then stretch a rubber band around one of the line holders to fix the depth. This prevents your line from unwinding too far, so you can quickly return your bait to the precise depth after catching a fish.

4. PULL the cord when you see the float move. You can bring the fish up quickly; a 1-foot pull on the cord will retrieve about 4 feet of line. Grab the smelt to keep it from dropping back into the hole. It may have the bait in its teeth but not be hooked.

Burbot

Most ice anglers won't crown the burbot the prettiest fish to grace the ice, and their habit of wrapping their long, slimy tails around an angler's arm while hooks are being removed has made more than one ice angler cringe. Yet burbot, also commonly called eelpout or lawyers, are found throughout a good portion of the North American ice-fishing region and, prepared correctly, offer flavor many compare to cod or haddock.

Burbot can be found in the cool waters of the Great Lakes, a number of river systems, most notably the Mississippi, and their river associated lakes, backwa-

ters and tributaries. They have also been stocked in some inland waters as a means of controlling over-populated panfish. Unlike most species of fish, burbot actually spawn during midwinter beneath the ice on shallow sand and gravel flats.

Burbot can easily be identified by their elongated, yellow-brown bodies mottled with dark brown or black markings, large, tough jaws and long dorsal and anal fins that extend from the fish's midsection right through to their long, wiggling, tapering tail sections. They eat virtually anything, including small fish, freshwater shrimp and other invertebrates.

In early winter, burbot frequent deep mud or gravel flats and their associated steep breaks lining vast shallow flats, where they move into shallower water at night to feed, and hold deeper during daylight hours. During midwinter, burbot spawn on shallow sand, gravel and rock reefs, points, shoals, and feed heavily in these same areas and along the drop-offs connecting these spots to deep water. By late season, burbot inhabit the deep edges of sharp-breaking, hard-bottom reefs, shoals, humps, points, flats and deep-water holes.

Burbot feed most intensely for several hours after sunset and again just before sun-up, but fished in the right areas, will feed sporadically throughout the entire evening. Most action occurs just around the spawning period as schools of burbot move up onto mid-depth humps, or better yet, up massive, deep-breaking main-lake points extending from deep water to large, shallow and mid-depth flats.

HOW TO CATCH BURBOT

Since burbot can be quite active beneath the ice, they're most often caught by ice anglers fishing live minnows on tip-ups or bobber rigs on jig rods. They're most commonly caught on or very near the bottom, often in depths exceeding 20 feet.

Standard dacron lines, monofilament leaders and minnow-tipped hooks account for many burbot catches, and since such standard riggings are commonly used for walleyes, pike and trout, surprising incidental catches of burbot are not unusual among anglers targeting other species.

While basic slip-bobber rigs and minnows probably account for the majority of the burbot iced each winter, phosphorescent (glow-in-the-dark) spoons and jigs tipped with a small minnow or minnow head can be deadly, depending on the fish's mood. Either way, contact with the bottom is important.

Gentle lift-drops composed of lifting your bait a few inches off bottom followed by a quick, slack-line-forming drop of the bait to

bottom and a brief pause is the key. If you lift your rod to repeat the motion and feel weight, set the hook. Many times burbot will suck in a jig without a violent hit or distinct thump.

Since most burbot are lost at the hole, be patient, making sure the fish's head is turned before attempting to slide the fish onto the ice. Burbot are strong and slippery, so the use of a gaff or carefully placed skimmer to guide the fish up can be helpful.

The International Eelpout Festival

Many ice anglers might believe the lowly burbot isn't a real attraction, but residents in the small, north-central Minnesota town of Walker will argue. Each year in the second weekend of February, the annual "International Eelpout Festival" draws thousands of local and visiting burbot anglers onto the ice of Leech Lake, a massive body of water known nationally for its tremendous walleye and muskie fishing. The tournament, which began in the late 1970's as more or less a joke, has turned into a major event and probably brought more attention to this species than any other promotion anywhere in the world.

The festival begins at noon on Friday and runs until noon Sunday. As expected, most of the eelpout are caught during the evening hours Friday and Saturday night. Even though the temperatures often dip below 0°F., many eelpout fisherman stay out on the ice all night long trying to catch the festival's biggest eelpout. Most years it takes a fish weighing 12 to 13 pounds to take top honors.

113

White Bass, Yellow Bass and White Perch

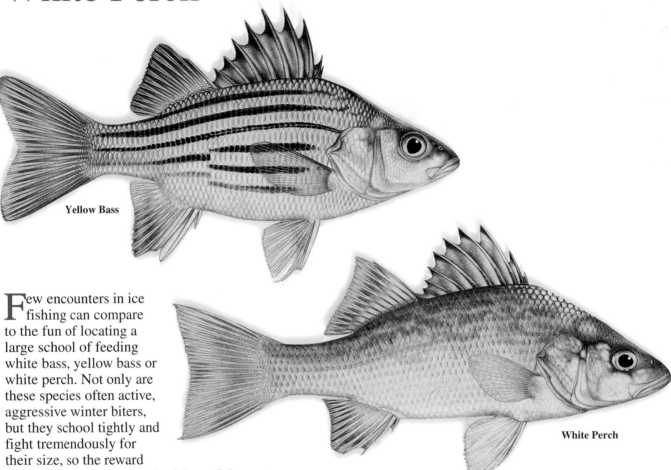

Yellow Bass

White Perch

Few encounters in ice fishing can compare to the fun of locating a large school of feeding white bass, yellow bass or white perch. Not only are these species often active, aggressive winter biters, but they school tightly and fight tremendously for their size, so the reward for locating a feeding pack of these fish creates experiences dedicated ice anglers never forget.

Known as the temperate basses of the ice-fishing world, white bass, yellow bass and white perch follow remarkably close habitat preferences and feeding habits. They're best identified by their distinctive, obvious side markings, as follows:

White bass (opposite page) are the most widely distributed of the three species, found in many natural lakes, reservoirs and river backwaters. White bass have silvery-white colored flanks featuring continuous horizontal black stripes along the upper sides, with the stripes dissipating toward the tail.

Yellow bass (above) closely resemble white bass, but are a pale, golden-yellow color and the horizontal black stripes along the sides are broken rather than continuous. While stocked in some natural lakes, they're more typically found in river systems and river reservoirs.

White perch (above) are shaped similarly to the white and yellow bass, but feature silvery-yellow sides lacking stripes.

Historically a brackish water species found mostly in estuaries along the Atlantic coast, stocking in some parts of the northeast United States has created landlocked populations of freshwater fish.

All three species are very active in winter, feeding on almost any available forage, including plankton, insect larvae, worms, crustaceans and small minnows.

HABITAT AND FEEDING PATTERNS

All three species flourish in large natural lakes, reservoirs and river backwaters, but may be found in smaller waters. They prefer moderately clear water with hard bottoms, and usually suspend in large conglomerations over mid-depth waters adjoining deep humps and shoals or deep holes.

White bass, yellow bass and white perch may feed virtually any time, day or night, but many anglers believe overcast, low-light and evening bites are most intense.

White bass caught on a jigging minnow

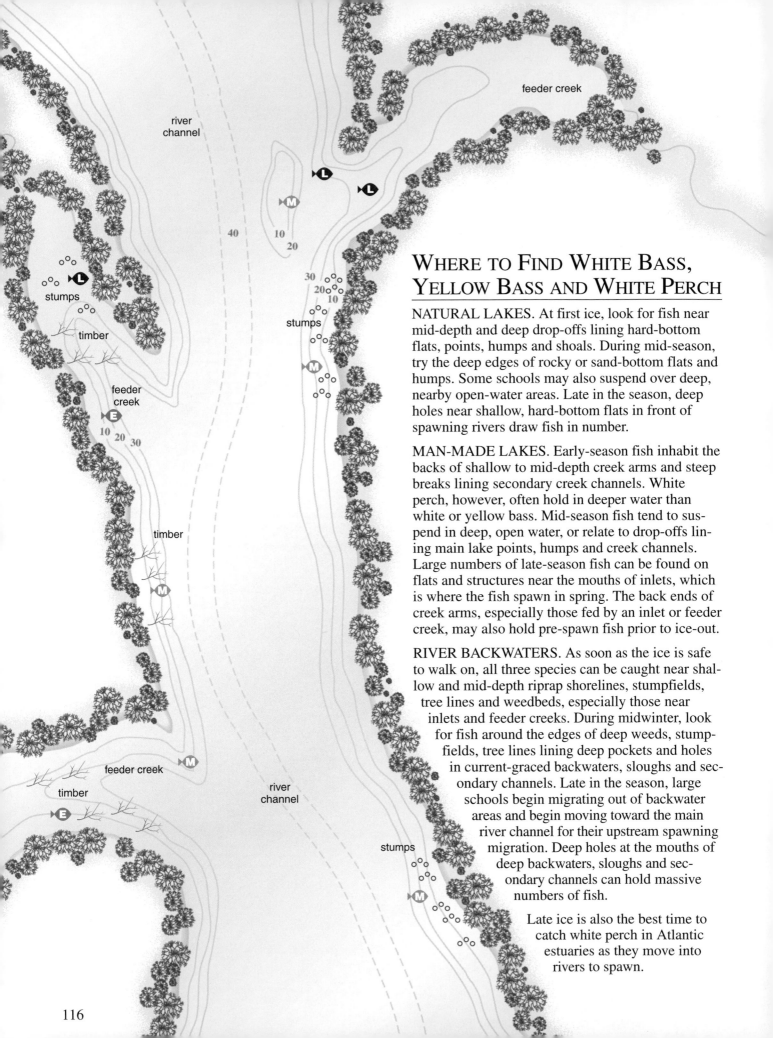

river channel

feeder creek

40   10
      20

30
20
10

stumps

stumps

timber

feeder
creek

10 20 30

timber

timber

feeder creek

timber

river
channel

stumps

WHERE TO FIND WHITE BASS, YELLOW BASS AND WHITE PERCH

NATURAL LAKES. At first ice, look for fish near mid-depth and deep drop-offs lining hard-bottom flats, points, humps and shoals. During mid-season, try the deep edges of rocky or sand-bottom flats and humps. Some schools may also suspend over deep, nearby open-water areas. Late in the season, deep holes near shallow, hard-bottom flats in front of spawning rivers draw fish in number.

MAN-MADE LAKES. Early-season fish inhabit the backs of shallow to mid-depth creek arms and steep breaks lining secondary creek channels. White perch, however, often hold in deeper water than white or yellow bass. Mid-season fish tend to suspend in deep, open water, or relate to drop-offs lining main lake points, humps and creek channels. Large numbers of late-season fish can be found on flats and structures near the mouths of inlets, which is where the fish spawn in spring. The back ends of creek arms, especially those fed by an inlet or feeder creek, may also hold pre-spawn fish prior to ice-out.

RIVER BACKWATERS. As soon as the ice is safe to walk on, all three species can be caught near shallow and mid-depth riprap shorelines, stumpfields, tree lines and weedbeds, especially those near inlets and feeder creeks. During midwinter, look for fish around the edges of deep weeds, stumpfields, tree lines lining deep pockets and holes in current-graced backwaters, sloughs and secondary channels. Late in the season, large schools begin migrating out of backwater areas and begin moving toward the main river channel for their upstream spawning migration. Deep holes at the mouths of deep backwaters, sloughs and secondary channels can hold massive numbers of fish.

Late ice is also the best time to catch white perch in Atlantic estuaries as they move into rivers to spawn.

How to Catch White Bass, Yellow Bass and White Perch

With white bass, yellow bass and white perch so active beneath the ice and feeding so heavily on many different types of forage, a variety of tactics are effective.

TIP-UPS. Cross member, underwater and thermal tip-ups set with standard minnow rigs all account for excellent winter catches, and wind tip-ups rigged with minnow-tipped flutter spoons or jigs are becoming an increasingly popular means of taking these aggressive winter feeders.

Tip-ups are especially popular among ice experts pursuing white bass. Standard dacron rigged with a long 6-pound-test leader and small minnow-tipped hook account for most catches. Most anglers simply scatter their tip-ups along deep breaks and at various depths in nearby open water, using them to locate schools and the most productive depth to fish.

When setting your tip-ups, try using a three-way swivel rigged with two dropper lines of different lengths spiced with colored beads or flicker blades leading to #4 hooks tipped with lip-hooked minnows.

The benefits of such dropper rigs allow you to effectively fish two separate depths, and the beads or blades often attract a fish and bring a strike. When a flag trips, however, take your time when coming to set the hook. With double-hook rigs, white bass often strike so hard they commonly hook themselves on one line, and as the hooked fish runs, the second line is dragged behind, often inspiring a strike from a second fish in the school.

JIGGING. A light to medium-light action rod combo with 4- to 8-pound monofilament and simple slip-bobber rig probably catches more winter white bass, yellow bass and white perch than any other technique.

Still, when white bass are fussy, small, grub-tipped ice jigs such as teardrops, ants, rockers and fish eyes fished with a finesse-style jigging approach will help increase your catch. Mid-size ice jigs packed with maggots or tipped with a small minnow and worked with a subtle lift-drop method is a popular way of instigating strikes under less than ideal conditions.

Should you find the white bass active, heavier, flashier spoons, swimming jigs, bladebaits and jigging minnows that drop down fast are a more efficient means of taking fish before the school moves or settles. With any of these baits, a more aggressive walleye-style snap- or rip-jigging technique is usually most effective.

Jigging with a number of flashy, bait-tipped jigs, spoons, bladebaits and jigging minnows is especially productive when fishing active, fast-moving schools, and with the nonstop action of such fish congregations, ice anglers using these methods are rarely able to fish two lines at the same time.

If you mark schools of white bass during the day but experience limited success, try coming back after dark when they often rise higher in the water column and feed aggressively. Many night-bite white bass anglers have found drilling two holes and setting a gas lantern in between them is a good way to draw active fish. Bobber rigs or lure and minnow presentations have both proven effective.

Lastly, if you're catching white bass but find they're mostly small fish, don't waste your time waiting for bigger fish to start hitting. White bass school by age and therefore size, so when the catch is small, you're best off to move in search of a school comprised of larger fish.

Bay De Noc Swedish Pimple

Shearwater Tackle Ant Jig

System Tackle Flyer

Reef Runner Cicada

Nils Master Jigger

Mid-depth flats or creek channels and their drop-offs supporting green weeds are primary targets early and late season, with the steepest breaking sections of main-lake points and bars being best during mid-season. Still, largemouth can be hard to find, especially on large lakes with lots of deep water.

Small ponds and pits featuring less deep water are better targets for finding concentrations of winter largemouth. Focus on shallow, weedy flats and drops early and late in the season, and the deep, weedy edges of main-lake points extending from the shallows to the deepest available water during mid-season.

Most winter largemouth experts prefer to fish during low-light or overcast conditions, when largemouth are most likely to roam and feed.

Some largemouth are taken on lightly set underwater tip-ups and tip-downs on light monofilament rigs and small fathead or shiner minnows. Set the trip too heavy, use too much weight or a minnow that's too large, and they're likely to drop the bait before you can set the hook.

Light and medium-light action spinning ice combos rigged with 4- to 6-pound monofilament and size 4 or 6 rocker jigs, tube jigs, teardrops and ice flies dressed with small minnows or maggots are good bets, although small spoons, bladebaits or jigging minnows tipped with minnow heads can also be effective. A lightweight flutter spoon with a short dropper to a hooked minnow, for example, is an excellent winter largemouth bait.

Precise jigging is critical, and productive methods may range from slow, methodical lift-drops to fast snap-jigs, depending on the fish's mood. Regardless of technique, however, fish lightweight, small lures tipped with fresh bait, keep your hooks sharp and, if you feel a take, set the hook immediately. Largemouth are infamously known to mouth and quickly drop winter baits.

Largemouth Bass

During spring, summer and fall, largemouth bass are the number-one gamefish throughout much of North America. In winter, because largemouth are not active winter feeders, they're virtually forgotten. Still, some ice experts have found targeting largemouths fun, especially during early and late winter, when largemouth are most easily caught.

Largemouth feature light greenish-yellow sides with a dark lateral streak down their side, and as their name implies, large, cavernous mouths. They feed sparingly beneath the ice on insect larvae, crustaceans and minnows.

Winter largemouth are characteristically deep, weed-dwelling fish in most natural lakes and reservoirs.

Smallmouth Bass

Like largemouth bass, smallmouth bass are all but ignored by most ice anglers. Nonetheless, smallmouth are available and willing to strike, especially during early and late winter.

Smallmouth boast greenish-golden-brown sides barred with dark vertical columns along their sides, and three dark bars radiating back from each eye. During the winter months they feed on insect larvae, crustaceans and minnows.

Winter smallmouth are typically deep-schooling, hard-bottom loving fish that congregate tightly in specific areas where forage is most densely concentrated. In small ponds and natural lakes, mid-depth and deep weedlines usually hold fish. On larger, deeper waters, deep holes, pockets and drops off main-basin rocky bars, shoals points, humps, rock piles or creek channels and any protrusions or indentations along their surrounding breaks are primary targets. In the late season, hard-bottom areas lining spring spawning flats and shoals can be productive.

Winter anglers targeting smallmouth believe fishing during low-light or overcast conditions produce best, unless dark water, thick ice or deep snow reduce the sun's glare. In such cases, smallmouth may feed best during midday.

Tip-ups are very effective for catching winter smallmouth. Try lightly set underwater tip-ups or tip-downs, light monofilament rigs with small minnows or hooks packed with wiggling grubs or maggots to attract bites, and add enough weight to access and hold your bait at the desired depth.

In addition to tip-ups, many smallmouth anglers use light to medium-light action spinning ice combos rigged with 4- to 6-pound monofilament and size 4 or 6 twister-tail-tipped leadhead jigs, tube jigs, ice flies or small flutter spoons dressed with small minnows or maggots. Heavy jigging spoons or blade-baits with droppers leading to a minnow, maggot or grub-hooked ice jig is another excellent combination, providing for quick drops into deep water, plenty of flash to draw fish, and a light, easy-to-strike meal once a fish gets there.

As when fishing winter largemouth, precise jigging is critical for smallmouth, with slow, methodical lift-drops and frequent pauses usually triggering the most strikes.

Releasing Fish

With increasingly sophisticated winter-fishing pressure being applied to our frozen waters, one of the most important contributions our generation of ice anglers can commit to is catch-and-release. Not only is this a voluntary practice by concerned ice anglers, but as ice fishing continues to increase in popularity, catch-and-release is also becoming increasingly important as a sound fish management tool for biologists.

Many modern ice anglers follow a practice called "selective harvest," meaning the number of kept fish is reduced to only a small quantity of small- to mid-size fish and an occasional trophy. This ensures the survival of mature, mid-size and large fish that most contribute to successful spawning.

Yet such catch-and-release practices are dependent on proper fish handling. Winter fish are better candidates for survival than summer ones, simply because cold water typically holds more oxygen and the cold temperatures also lower the fish's metabolism, which in turn lessens the overall amount of stress from being caught. Still, mishandled fish don't survive, which negates the benefit of these practices in the first place. Following is a listing of guidelines leading to successful winter catch-and-release.

TIPS FOR RELEASING FISH

• Land fish quickly rather than tiring them, then quickly remove the hooks, turn the fish around and release the fish back down the hole. Unless air temperatures are severely cold, handle your catch gently rather than hurriedly. Cold air and the fish's reduced metabolism enable fish to survive up to several minutes out of water, provided temperatures aren't extreme, when the risk of freezing sensitive tissues such as the eyes and gill filaments are increased, blinding the fish or reducing the fish's ability to absorb oxygen, respectively. Either diminishes the fish's chances of survival.

• Fish with artificial lures tipped with bait rather than solely live bait. Studies have demonstrated 50% mortality among fish caught on live bait, compared to 5% of those taken on artificial lures. While even deep-hooked fish stand a better chance of survival in cold water, fish hooked deeply and bleeding, especially from the gills, stand a lesser chance of successful release.

• Use artificial lures with single hooks and diminished or flattened barbs to lessen the amount of time it takes to unhook fish.

• Avoid Swedish hooks (right), which have been shown to promote deep hooking, when rigging dead baitfish under tip-ups.

• Use the lightest wire hooks possible when rigging with live bait. This way if hooks are swallowed you can simply cut your line, leaving the fish's digestive acids to disintegrate the hook with minimal harm to the fish.

• Leave a caught fish in the water at the top of the hole and remove the hooks with a needle-nose pliers. If you must hold the fish, do so with wet neoprene gloves. Touching fish with dry hands, gloves or mitts removes protective "slime," promoting bacterial and fungal growth.

• Lift fish carefully for photographs, supporting their full body weight with two wet hands, one positioned beneath the belly and the other placed in front of the tail. Never hold fish intended for release vertically by the jaw or lift them by the eye sockets. Rather, gently cradle fish by the belly and hold them in a horizontal position.

• Always handle fish gently during release, carefully suspending their heads in the water until they swim back down the hole. Never move fish back and forth in the hole to forcefully resuscitate them. Fish must bring water in through their mouths and over the gills in order to properly breathe.

The most important rule to keep in mind when practicing catch-and-release is to use common sense. Don't rip hooks out hastily, drop fish intended for release, nor allow them to flop around on the ice. By treating your favorite fish with respect, following regulations and properly releasing a portion of your catch, you will be helping maintain quality ice fishing for many generations to come.

Anglers releasing a lake trout back to the depths

Keeping Fish

Even in today's world of catch-and-release, most ice anglers will admit they practice selective catch-and-release, allowing them to enjoy occasional fish fries.

If it's convenient and weather conditions allow, maximum flavor can be attained by cleaning and preparing your fish right on the ice; many winter anglers experienced in such endeavors fondly refer to these feedings as "off-shore lunches." Few meals taste better.

When immediate food preparation isn't practical or convenient, caring for your catch to maintain good flavor begins with keeping fish alive so they remain fresh after being caught. In summer, keeping your fish cool is the ultimate challenge; in winter, preventing freezing is the ticket, and the best way to achieve this is to keep your fish alive. While you can use a stringer dipped below the ice for short-term storage, the best way to keep fish alive is by

creating a livewell on the ice (left).

To make such a livewell, begin by drilling several closely placed holes as far into the ice as possible, but without breaking through. Next, chisel the ice separating the holes to create a large tub and drill a hole directly alongside the tub until you break water. Finally, using your chisel, puncture a hole through the upper portion of the wall separating your tub from the water source hole, and allow the tub to fill with water. Presto, instant livewell!

When it's time to go ashore, place your catch in a cooler or plastic bag. But don't pack the cooler or bag with ice, snow or fill it with water—doing so only makes the fish more slimy and difficult to handle for cleaning. Likewise, if one or more fish expire on the stringer or in the livewell before it's time to quit fishing, get them out of the water and into an empty cooler.

Freezing Fish

If you plan to keep your fish for long-term storage, freeze your catch immediately after cleaning. Divide the meat into serving-size fillets, steaks or pieces as desired, then mix 2 tablespoons of ascorbic acid (available in drugstores) with 1 quart water. Briefly place fish in the mixture before submerging them in small, water-filled plastic containers, packing just enough meat for a meal in each, then freeze these blocks within the container.

Once frozen, remove your fish from the freezer, run cold water along the container bottom to loosen the frozen

block, remove it and wrap in a tightly sealed, double wrapping of freezer paper covered with aluminum foil before long-term freezing. The combination of ice, paper and foil virtually eliminates air contact, the leading cause of freezer burn.

When ready to prepare your meal, never thaw fish at room temperature. Rather, place the package in a sealed plastic bag, and soak the bag in refrigerated, cold water. Within 24 hours, your fish will be thawed in a fresh state, ready for cooking.

Index

Creative Publishing international is the most complete source of How-To Information for the Outdoorsman

THE COMPLETE HUNTER™ *Series*

- *White-tailed Deer*
- *Dressing & Cooking Wild Game*
- *Advanced Whitetail Hunting*
- *Bowhunting Equipment & Skills*
- *Understanding Whitetails*
- *Venison Cookery*
- *Muzzleloading*
- *Wild Turkey*
- *Duck Hunting*
- *America's Favorite Wild Game Recipes*
- *Upland Game Birds*
- *The Complete Guide to Hunting*
- *Game Bird Cookery*
- *North American Game Birds*
- *North American Game Animals*

The Freshwater Angler™ *Series*

- *Largemouth Bass*
- *The New Cleaning & Cooking Fish*
- *Fishing Tips & Tricks*
- *Trout*
- *Panfish*
- *All-Time Favorite Fish Recipes*
- *Fishing for Catfish*
- *Fishing With Artificial Lures*
- *Successful Walleye Fishing*
- *Advanced Bass Fishing*
- *The Art of Fly Tying*
- *The Art of Freshwater Fishing*
- *Fishing Rivers & Streams*
- *Northern Pike & Muskie*
- *Freshwater Gamefish of North America*
- *Fishing With Live Bait*
- *Fly Fishing for Trout in Streams*

The Complete FLY FISHERMAN™ *Series*

- *Fly-Tying Techniques & Patterns*
- *Fly-Fishing Equipment & Skills*
- *Fishing Nymphs, Wet Flies & Streamers – Subsurface Techniques for Trout in Streams*
- *Fishing Dry Flies – Surface Presentations for Trout in Streams*

Contributing Photographers (Note: T=*Top*, C=*Center*, B=*Bottom*, L=*Left*, R=*Right*, I=*Inset*)

Dave Genz
St. Cloud, MN
© *Dave Genz: back cover TL, p. 63*

Mike Hehner
Coon Rapids, MN
© *Mike Hehner: p. 4B*

Mark Kayser
Pierre, SD
© *Mark Kayser: pp. 21B, 22*

Bill Lindner Photography
St. Paul, MN
© *Bill Lindner: cover, back cover: TR, CR,
BR, pp. 4-5, 6-7, 8T, 8B, 16, 18, 19, 20-21,
23, 24-25, 27BL, 29BL, 29BR, 31I, 36T, 37C,
40L, 40R, 40-41 background, 41TL, 41BL,
42L, 43TL, 43C, 44, 45BR, 46TL, 46BL, 46R,
48TR, 48-49, 54-55, 61, 62T, 62B, 69, 70BR,
71, 71I, 78, 79T, 79B, 84T, 85T, 85B, 90T,
90B, 91, 92T, 98, 101, 112, 120, 122, 123*

Steve Maas
East Bethel, MN
© *Steve Maas: pp. 41R, 113*

Jim Schollmeyer
Salem, OR
© *Jim Schollmeyer: p. 107*

Contributing Illustrators

Maynard Reece
Des Moines, IA
© *Maynard Reece: p. 103T*

Joseph R. Tomelleri
Leawood, KS
© *Joseph R. Tomelleri: pp. 64, 73, 87, 94,
103BC, 103 coho, 103 chinook, 114 both*

Jon Q. Wright/Aqua Images
Minneapolis, MN
© *Jon Q. Wright/Aqua Images: pp. 57,
99 all, 103 landlocked*

– Editor's Note –

In addition to thanking the author, Tom Gruenwald, for his work in producing *Modern Methods of Ice
Fishing,* special thanks must go to Tom's employer, **HT Enterprises, Inc.,** for their cooperation.

Since 1978, HT Enterprises, Inc. has supplied sporting goods stores with top-quality ice tackle for the ice-
fishing enthusiast. While many anglers are familiar with HT's unbeatable selection of tip-ups, the company
also makes a wide variety of rods, reels, lines, lures and accessories for both winter and summer fishing.

For more information contact HT at the addresses and numbers listed below:

HT Enterprises, Inc.
P.O. Box 909 Campbellsport, WI 53010

• phone: *(920) 533-5080* • fax: *(920) 533-5147* • e-mail: *htent@excel.net*